Marine Mysteries and Dramatic Disasters
of New England

Marine Mysteries
and Dramatic Disasters
of New England

EDWARD ROWE SNOW

ILLUSTRATED

DODD, MEAD & COMPANY, NEW YORK

Library of Congress Cataloging in Publication Data

Snow, Edward Rowe.
  Marine mysteries and dramatic disasters of New England.

  Includes index.
  1. Disasters—New England. 2. Shipwrecks—New England.
3. New England—History—Miscellanea.
I. Title.
F4.6.S66   974   76–28985
ISBN 0–396–07378–6

To Victoria Zehringer Snow

ACKNOWLEDGMENTS

Various institutions aided me in my research including the Boston Atheneum, the Boston Public Library, the Bostonian Society, and the Massachusetts Archives.

Many individuals gave me freely of their ability and time. Some have asked for and have been given anonymity. Others whom I wish to mention are:

Dorothy Snow Bicknell, Laura Ann Bicknell, Richard Carlisle, Frederick G. S. Clow, Arthur Cunningham, James Douglas, Walter Spahr Ehrenfeld, Jean Foley, Suzanne Flandreau, Robert Grunin, Marie Hanson, Melina Herron, Dorothy Haegg Jacobson, Trevor Johnson, Joseph Kolb, Larry Molignano, Richard Nakashian, Joel O'Brien, William Pyne, Elva Ruiz, Helen Salkowski, Frederick Sanford, Chester Shea, Alfred Schroeder, William Smits, Donald B. Snow, Barbara Urbanowitz, Ann Wadsworth, Susan Williams.

John R. Herbert, prominent Quincy newsman and banker, assisted me in several difficult stories. As he has done for more than a quarter century, he helped solve many of the problems that the writing of the book involved.

Anna-Myrle Snow, my faithful wife and fellow researcher,

gave me many hours of assistance in the preparation of this book in spite of her deep involvement in tennis.

EDWARD ROWE SNOW
Marshfield, Massachusetts
May 1976

CONTENTS

PART THREE: At Sea

ILLUSTRATIONS

PART ONE

Along the Waterfront

CHAPTER 1

~~~~~~

THE BRINK'S HOLDUP

On the evening of January 17, 1950, shortly after seven o'clock, masked bandits stole more than $2,000,000 in checks, bonds, and currency from the North End headquarters of Brink's Incorporated on Prince Street in Boston, Massachusetts. Delivering cash for payrolls and returning the day's receipts to Brink's were the most important tasks of the company.

The Prince Street building, located close to the waterfront and harbor across from the frigate *Constitution*, was considered an impenetrable stronghold. From the front entrance a series of locked doors led to a cement vault where the money was kept.

At the time, the Brink's robbery was the greatest holdup in American history and excited the imagination of people all over the world.

The very first thought concerning the Brink's holdup was born in the mind of Tony Pino, a middle-aged ruffian of Boston's North End. One day he was watching the regularity with which scores of armored trucks with armed guards daily entered and left the Brink's garage at 165 Prince Street, at the corner of Prince and Commercial Streets. Then Pino began

3

visiting various locations in which the Brink's trucks were often seen. He watched the ease with which the guards handled thousands of dollars in cash, almost always acting with the relative nonchalance that people accustomed to handling money show to those of us who never have and never will be able to assume that matter-of-fact attitude.

Later Pino took to acquainting himself with residents of apartments or tenements overlooking the Brink's building. Occasionally he would be invited to the roofs on hot nights or at other times. These visits gave him an excuse to observe what was going on at Brink's while remaining inconspicuous. When surveying the Brink's garage entrance and the other doors that led into the building, he observed carefully the time those employed there entered and the time they left.

Then came the day he believed himself ready for the first physical move of his plan. It would be a continuous operation that was actually never to end until the great theft was carried out. Pino organized a criminal band of Boston area crooks second to none. The men he interviewed would maim, kill, and act relentlessly toward other humans whenever the occasion required. Those in the group were to be held together by strong underworld agreements and forged into a single unit that had but a single objective—to steal more than a million dollars!

People in the North End have told me that Pino began his crooked life as a child by stealing coal. Later he renewed his close friendship with the boyhood chums who thought as he did. He eventually concentrated on two men, Stan Gusciora and Specs O'Keefe, who had been brought up in similar fashion in the tenement districts of Boston.

Gusciora, or Gus, as he was known, was quicker in action and had a tougher manner, while Specs was acknowledged to be the smartest of the three.

Taking the two men to the scene of their future crime, Pino

showed them details of the building that housed Brink's Incorporated, and his crude charts of the coming and going of the many employees. Specs later admitted that the very audacious brashness of Pino's plan staggered him, but after careful consideration, he decided that he would accept the general scheme Pino outlined. Nevertheless, Specs O'Keefe believed that certain changes would have to be made, and he planned the robbery in a substantially different manner from Pino.

Pino had suggested two possible methods of operation. The first had the planners hiding at night in the building itself, where they could overcome the employees who would enter the edifice the next morning. The other possibility that Pino considered was to grab the Brink's head cashier and use his knowledge to open the vault.

O'Keefe was not too fond of either method. To investigate further, he and his friend Gus began roaming around outside the building at times when they were not apt to get caught. They gradually accumulated knowledge of astonishing importance. Finally they were able to enter this modern treasure citadel in the North End with no more bother than burglars have getting into a house in the suburbs! Not only could they enter the sprawling establishment with the greatest of ease, but they discovered that when they were ready to leave they were able to vanish in the same inconspicuous manner.

One night they experimented and found they could get into the garage adjoining the treasure house simply by manipulating the lock with an ice pick. Once inside, by inserting a piece of celluloid in a second lock, they successfully opened the door into the main building. After stepping inside, tense and alert, they expected to hear alarm bells ringing and other security measures thwarting their further attempts at entrance. They waited as the minutes passed. Absolutely nothing occurred.

Then quietly, for they had donned rubbers to reduce the

sound of their footsteps, they walked along the corridor. Soon the criminals reached the vault room itself, where the two most interesting items they noticed were a tally board and a burglar alarm system. In reconnoitering in this way, they discovered that they would need to solve the problem of the alarm system before there was any chance of their being able to accomplish their purpose.

Night after night, according to Specs O'Keefe, the gang visited the interior of the Brink's building until they became thoroughly familiar with the layout and the problems they might encounter. They learned that a few minutes after seven each night the cashiers in the vault room set the switch of the automatic alarm. Soon the crooks in their nocturnal visits began the habit of carefully studying the tally board, which recorded each day's receipts, and realized that it often registered more than a million dollars!

Wondering how they might nullify the effects of the alarm, the prospective thieves figured that if they could remove even for a few hours the lock cylinders from each successive door all the distance from the front of the building to the vault room itself, have keys made, and replace the locks without detection, there would be no trouble with the alarm. One night they took away the cylinders, visited a locksmith who cut keys for them, and returned the cylinders before the morning workers arrived. The thieves were able to solve the problem of the final lock in the series, but they never revealed how.

Finally, with all in readiness, the crooks decided that January 17 would be the date for the burglary. According to their plan, seven men would enter together. Breaking through to the vault, they would tie up the cashiers and take the money. Two others would wait outside in a truck to transport the actual robbers away from the scene of the theft. Another man would be on top of a nearby roof ready to warn if danger came. The eleventh crook, Joe McGinnis, would meet the others at a hideout and take over all the money.

A stolen, green three-quarter-ton Ford truck, chauffeurs' uniforms, navy jackets, Halloween masks, and special rope for tying up the cashiers comprised the equipment they had ready for that evening.

On Tuesday night, January 17, 1950, a drizzle was falling, which was ideal for the gangsters. The operation began when the seven men arrived at the Brink's building. Their outfits were such that they would have been taken for ordinary employees. Specs O'Keefe stood briefly at the front door of the building at 165 Prince Street. Casually he opened the door with his recently-made key, and the seven crooks filed inside. Then every man paused to don his Halloween mask, each ready for whatever lay ahead.

Shortly after seven o'clock that evening, cashier Thomas Lloyd was working as usual checking the money at the vault. Four other colleagues were with him: James Allen, a veteran bank worker with more than twenty-two years of experience, Sherman Smith, Herman Pfaff, and Charles Grell. Then came that moment of incredible drama at about ten minutes after seven. Seven bandits appeared before the five employees.

"Five of us were in the vault and the outer cage near the vault," Allen later explained in an interview with me. "Seven men, all of medium size and armed, wearing masks, walked into the back of the vault and right up to the cage. One of them spoke to us.

" 'We'll let you have it if you move.' I heard the others talking but their voices were far too low to understand.

"The vault door, leading out into the cage, was filled with cash, checks, negotiable securities, and coin. The inner door was open, and there was a substantial amount on the cage floor. They made us open the cage door itself and then roughed us up a little. One of them ripped off my glasses. They pushed us down on the floor and not too gently snatched our pistols away. They then tied us up, plastering adhesive tape across our mouths."

Within a short time the seven bandits put more than a million dollars into two giant Federal Reserve Bank bags, cursing because the actual weight of the currency prevented their carrying the coins along also. The coins, in fact, were worth another million dollars.

Eighteen minutes later the seven bandits quietly left the building. There still is controversy as to whether or not they were hurried by the sounding of a buzzer immediately before they fled the Brink's establishment, but in any case, they stepped into two cars and sped away into oblivion.

A few minutes later the Brink's guards untied themselves and notified the police authorities of the gigantic robbery. Pandemonium broke loose, and as soon as it was physically possible Boston Police Superintendent Edward W. Fallon took over. Ordering 150 policemen—captains, lieutenants, sergeants, and detectives—to assemble at headquarters, Fallon explained that this Brink's crime was actually a climax to a series of 1949 and 1950 robberies.

Superintendent Fallon told the others in detail what had taken place and emphasized the vital necessity for solving this gigantic, overwhelming robbery, the largest haul in the history of America.* He stated that the money had been taken from payrolls and receipts of many substantial firms, and that in their haste the thieves had overlooked $880,000 consigned to

---

* The previous record for armed robbery was held by bandits who on August 21, 1934, took $427,000 from an armored bank truck while the guards were picking up $25,000 from the Rubel Ice Corporation plant in Brooklyn, New York. Boston's only comparable holdup was at the B. F. Sturtevant plant in Hyde Park, where a payroll valued at $115,000 was taken. The second greatest Boston loss had been $29,000 at the American Sugar Refinery in South Boston.

the General Electric Company and $120,000 belonging to Filene's department store.

Evidently the timing under which the crooks operated was accurate to the closest degree. They had chosen a moment when all Brink's drivers had reported in, parked their cars in the huge gloomy cavern of the first floor garage, made their financial adjustments with the cashiers, and then left for the night.

Upstairs where the gigantic cement vault, impregnable if closed and locked, was located, the five workers had been counting funds and transferring them into envelopes. The physical arrangement of the building was believed to provide maximum security, but, of course, the robbery itself nullified this theory.

Two days later a telephone call coming from New Jersey from a never-identified man who claimed to be a driver of one of the get-away cars asserted that all the money had been hidden "within a minute's drive of the holdup scene." This message sent squads of policemen to the North End within a few hours, and many areas were searched, but in vain.

Boston banks were quick to assure the public that in spite of this greatest theft in the nation's history, the robbery took away only one dollar for every $2700 normally in circulation in the Boston Reserve District in 1950, a total of $2,700,000,000.

The first phase of the Brink's affair was rapidly drawing to a close. Soon, except for an occasional mention, the robbery disappeared from the front page of the Boston papers, and the public turned to other matters of interest.

For several years clues to the solution of the crime were few and far between. Even the fact that more than $98,000 of the loot was in bills whose serial numbers were known did little to solve the robbery.*

* There were ten $1000 bills, a hundred $100 bills, forty fifties, and 400 twenties, as well as 3400 tens, 3400 fives, 1200 twos, and 15,000 ones that

But unfortunately for the criminals, as has been the case since time immemorial, the robbers who had been so successful in planning the robbery were not to be so lucky after the burglary had taken place. Individual greed seems to have been the major factor in the gradual loosening of the ties that up to the night of the robbery were so definite and binding.

As it happened, every one of the eleven men involved in the robbery was among those picked up for the customary questioning, but all eleven were released. By this time the loot had been divided. Each member of the gang received $100,000, the exact amount of the reward offered for their detection.

Specs O'Keefe stored his $100,000 overnight with a "friend." Returning in less than twenty-four hours, he counted the money again only to discover that it had shrunk to $98,000 in one day! He took what was left away with him, putting $5,000 aside for his own expenses and hiding $93,000 at the home of Adolph Maffie. As matters turned out, Specs never saw any of the $93,000 again. With Stanley Gusciora he fled to Pennsylvania, where the two stole pistols, bullets, and clothes. Arrested for those thefts, they were convicted and imprisoned for several years.

Back in Boston, $380,000 of the loot had been stored in a covered basket. When opened after an interval of time it contained exactly $345,000! The person who had guarded the basket barely saved himself from being shot to death at once at the order of Specs O'Keefe by claiming that when the police put him under surveillance he stored the cash with a friend and thus could not be held responsible.

The police searched diligently for the slightest clue to the

---

made up the known bills. The stolen money included silver certificates of the 1935–C issues, and the exact numbers of 50 of the one dollar bills from L–39152501 E to L–39153000 E.

Including the $98,000, the exact amount of money stolen was $1,218,211.29 in cash and $1,557,183.83 in checks and negotiable securities, for a total of $2,775,395.12.

robbery. Finally their efforts were rewarded. Fragments of the green Ford truck were discovered in a nearby dump, with the evidence indicating that a blowtorch and sledgehammer had been used in an attempt to destroy the car. It appeared that the criminals had tried to bury the truck remains, but hard frozen ground had thwarted their efforts. Week after week police detectives worked tracing down each major clue, until finally they had assembled enough disjointed facts to implicate eight of the eleven robbers.

Nevertheless, there was insufficient evidence to convict, and as the months passed, the FBI realized they needed more facts. They were especially frustrated because they knew that the Federal three-year statute of limitations would take effect in the first month of the following year.

During the waning weeks of 1952, the eight suspected holdup men were brought to one central location. Nevertheless, the year 1953 arrived, and the FBI did not have sufficient evidence to hold the criminals. On January 16, 1953, with one day remaining of the three-year statute of limitations that is Federal Law, the Grand Jury stated there simply wasn't enough evidence for a trial, and the eight men were not indicted. And so it was that at midnight the FBI transferred their efforts to aiding the state of Massachusetts, whose legal representatives could act for three years more under its six-year statute of limitations. J. Edgar Hoover made it clear that his organization would "never quit the Brink's Case." If the FBI cracked the mystery, Hoover emphasized, all the evidence would be turned over to Massachusetts.

After completing his Pennsylvania jail sentence in February 1954, Specs O'Keefe returned to Boston. To his consternation, he discovered that Adolph Maffie had spent practically every dollar of the $93,000 Specs had entrusted to him. It is a miracle that O'Keefe did not kill Maffie on the spot, but the latter promised substantial restitution.

Nevertheless, O'Keefe held Maffie prisoner, locked and tied up, while he decided what his next move might be. Maffie told him to see Pino. Keeping Maffie bound, O'Keefe went to Pino to ask Pino to advance him $25,000.

Specs waited several weeks for money and, as Pino did not provide him with any funds, Specs threatened Pino. Since the threats produced no results in the way of money, Specs kidnapped Vincent Costa, another gang member who was also Pino's brother-in-law. Pino now gave Specs $2500 and O'Keefe released Costa.

Retaliation against Specs by others in the gang was soon to follow, and the fact that O'Keefe stayed alive during the next few weeks says much for his sagacity, alertness, and agility. One day, while getting into his Oldsmobile, he noticed another car parked nearby. Then as he turned into a relatively narrow street, the strange car pulled up alongside and an occupant in the back seat began to spray Specs' car with bullets from a sub-machine gun. The moment the other car approached O'Keefe dropped down on the floor boards so that every bullet missed him.

A few weeks later his luck did not hold out. While parking his car, he was shot twice, sustaining a wound in the wrist and another in the chest. A physician who took care of gangland injuries kept him alive with penicillin. Specs recovered to begin serving a sentence of more than two years because of conviction for an earlier crime.

Officials in the FBI, who had never really lost track of O'Keefe's activities, decided to make a proposal to him. Two days after Christmas, two agents of the FBI visited O'Keefe in Hampton County Jail at Springfield, Massachusetts, where he had been incarcerated. They were still interested in the Brink's case, the FBI men explained, and they knew Specs was also interested. He might like to know that his old comrades were cashing in on their good fortune. His close friend Anthony

Pino had acquired a brand new residence, while his late associate Vincent Costa had invested in an automobile agency and was beginning to prosper. The FBI men then left to allow the message to penetrate O'Keefe's mental defenses, and a day or so later they made a return visit.

On January 6, 1956, almost six years after the Brink's robbery—but only ten days after their first visit—the two members of the FBI made a third call on Specs. The persuasive triple visits affected Specs in such fashion that his defenses collapsed and his surrender soon became complete. Deciding to tell everything he knew about his part in the robbery, Specs first revealed the entire list of those involved in the holdup of January 17, 1950. They were Henry Baker, Joseph S. Banfield, Vincent J. Costa, James I. Flaherty, Michael Geagan, Stanley Gusciora, Adolph Maffie, Joseph F. McGinnis, Joseph James O'Keefe, Anthony Pino, and Thomas F. Richardson.

Later, under the most dramatic security measures in Massachusetts history, Specs was removed from jail and escorted secretly under heavy guard to the office of District Attorney Garrett Byrne. There under merciless questioning, O'Keefe not only reiterated his complete account but also remembered a few extra details for good measure.

Just six days after O'Keefe's confession the blow fell for the surviving members of the Brink's gang. Two had died, but six members of the original eleven were arrested by the FBI. Stanley Gusciora was already in jail at the time. When he heard that Specs had "betrayed" him, he broke down and cried like a baby. Later that year he suddenly collapsed, and he died of a tumor a short time afterward.

It was not long after Stanley Gusciora's death that all members of the Brink's gang still alive were brought together for trial in Boston. On a warm September day in 1956 the trial began, and forty-five days later O'Keefe's comrades were sentenced to jail for life. District Attorney Byrne pleaded for clemency in the case of Specs, stating that O'Keefe should not get a life sentence. He emphasized the fact that both Massachusetts and the FBI would have been eternally embarrassed if it had not been for Spec's confession, and four years later, in November 1960, Specs O'Keefe was paroled. He was given a new identity. In the spring of 1976 he died of natural causes.

Did this crime pay? Everyone vitally concerned with its history is emphatic in stating that the Brink's robbery did not pay those who perpetrated it, but it did have certain fringe benefits for many of their immediate associates who profited substantially at the time.

Money from the robbery has been discovered in relatively miniscule amounts from time to time, but the bulk of the illegal treasure still eludes the authorities. On several occasions I have toured the North End of Boston in a vain attempt to discover what many others have failed to find, some of the more than $1,000,000 still missing from the famed Brink's holdup.

Often with my older brother, the late Winthrop James Snow, I would climb down around old musty brick walls, passageways, and arches, including the Captain James Gruchy tunnel * at 455 Commercial Street, later taken over by the Coast Guard. Win was an expert in the brick and tile industry and gave me many pointers on where and how the thieves might have secreted the major part of the cash, which so far has never been found.

* See my *True Tales of Buried Treasure* and C. L. Reeves' book *Captain Gruchy's Gambols.*

CHAPTER 2

THE MOLASSES DISASTER

While studying at Harvard University more than forty years ago I had drilled into my rather reluctant mind the importance of the economic triangle represented by molasses from the West Indies, slaves from Africa, and rum from Medford and Boston.

Molasses has always been a vital import into the port of Boston. Millions upon millions of gallons of the sticky, sweet liquid have been turned into candy and a spread for bread. Molasses has also been an ingredient in New England gingerbread and cookies. Moreover, the United States Industrial Alcohol Company, which ran the Purity Distilling Company in the North End of Boston, changed molasses into distilled alcohol.

The gigantic tank, 52 feet high and 91 feet in diameter, in which the United States Alcohol Company stored molasses in crude form was a prominent landmark of the North End waterfront area. This commercial neighborhood was dominated in the year 1919, as it is in 1976, by Copp's Hill Cemetery. In 1919, from the vantage point of the graveyard high on the hill, a person would have an outstanding view of the surrounding area to the north. He would see Bunker Hill Monument, the battleship *Constitution*, Commercial Street, the Public

Works Department of the City of Boston, the paving division of Boston, the Fire Station with Fireboat Engine 31, the warehouses of the Boston and Worcester Railway, the Eastern Massachusetts Railway, and in the immediate foreground, the trestle of the Boston Elevated tracks high in the air.

It is often said that half a century and more ago winters were colder than they are today, but in January 1919 the streets of Boston were nearly free of snow. Although there were a few days of chilly weather, several unexpectedly warm days arrived during the middle of that month. As Alton Hall Blackington expressed it in his book *Yankee Yarns*, it was so warm that the children of the North End "played marbles and danced on the sidewalk to the tunes of a hurdy-gurdy."

With noon approaching on January 15, it seemed like a real spring day. Men walked around without overcoats, and girls strolled bareheaded, enjoying the warmth of the unexpected weather.

At the Worcester freight terminal on the waterfront, Percy Smerage was checking leather bales, beer barrels, and potatoes. Four freight cars on which he had completed tallies, or counts, were fully loaded.

Suddenly there was a terrific noise "like a thousand machine guns" followed by an unbelievable roar as the enormous tank, containing 2,300,000 gallons of molasses, split into several sections. A veritable geyser of the yellowish brown liquid shot up into the air, and a river of molasses three times as high as a man billowed forth in all directions.

The heavy, sluggish, overwhelming torrent pushed its bulky way out from the tank, engulfing everything in its path. The loaded freight cars were picked up like fragments of wood in a tidal wave. A fifth freight car, only half filled, was pushed right through the wall of the railroad terminal. It was an awesome, unbelievable sight. The weight of the molasses dropped three workers and several horses down into the basement of the freight terminal, men and horses perishing together.

When the molasses hit the Boston Fire Station, the building was lifted from its foundation and battered against the harbor wharf pilings, killing three fire fighters of Fireboat 31. One of them, Engineer William Leahy, was crushed to death by a billiard table that literally flew through the air and smashed into him. The surviving fire fighters on duty labored long and heroically in spite of injuries, pulling victims from collapsed buildings and other scattered debris in the area.

An unidentified cadet from the training ship *Nantucket* rescued a woman from the third floor of a tenement. Alton Hall Blackington, photographing the rescue, slipped and fell into the molasses, but was successful in taking his pictures.

As witnesses described it later, the disaster began with a muffled roar and a "clangor of steel against steel and the crash of rending wood." However, the roar and the din were momentary. After the explosion great ribbons of thick, brownish fluid pushed everywhere, moving at the approximate rate of speed of heavy liquid cement. The huge tossing geyser simply overwhelmed any object which lay in its path, becoming what one expert later called an "adhesive flood." It inundated everyone and everything.

In a single stroke the force of the explosion tore the great tank apart, plate by plate. The outward shock was followed by a tremendous vacuum that actually pulled or sucked into rubble any nearby structure that was not damaged by the initial blast.

The steel plates, half an inch thick, were catapulted in every direction by the unleashed energy of the explosion. Crashing into the elevated trestle, the plates knifed through the steel girders that supported the tracks and the trains, missing one of several moving elevated cars by less than a hundred yards.

The outward force of the explosion forced a team of horses and a wagon from the pavements of the freight yards through a board fence, pushing them to the corner of Commercial and Charter Streets. Late that afternoon the carcasses of the horses were taken from the molasses ooze and removed from the area.

One example of individual suffering was that of Martin J. Clougherty. A prominent Boston sportsman, boxing referee, and manager of the Pen and Pencil Club, Clougherty lived at 6 Copp's Hill Terrace, the family home since 1872. The blast picked up his 69-year-old mother, Mrs. Bridget Clougherty, and blew her right through a window, killing her almost at once. The house itself was lifted in one piece from its underpinnings.

Mrs. Clougherty's son later told of his experience. "I could not sleep this morning before the explosion," stated Martin. "I wanted to get up and go out, and I don't know why. I wouldn't say it was a premonition. Anyway I'm glad I didn't go out. My dear old mother told me to sleep longer as I had put in three or four sleepless nights after refereeing bouts. I distinctly heard the rumbling which preceded the explosion.

"First I thought it was an elevated train on fire. Anyway, in less time than it takes to tell it I dreamed that I had found myself in the river and heavy weights were pressing on my chest.

"I must have had my mother's prayers with me for by some means I managed to extricate myself before I smothered to death. Indeed I thought that I had been thrown into the Charles River. I found my sister and dragged her out of the rubble, but I could not find my mother or my brother."

A huge powerful man, Martin Clougherty was seriously injured and suffered for several hours from shock. Mrs. Clougherty, who was in the kitchen when the blast shattered the house, died almost at once, although Clougherty's brother, who was also there, was only slightly injured when he was rescued.

The entire area was simply plastered with molasses—rooftops, trees, overhead wires, and grass plots were all covered with the sticky substance. Commercial Street was a river of molasses at least four feet deep.

Harry F. Dolan, attorney for the United States Industrial Alcohol Company, stated that the actual explosion may have come from an outside source. He was reasonably sure that the blast did not originate in either the tank or its contents. The tank, Dolan explained, was of the most modern construction, the maker more than reliable.

"The damage," said the attorney, "will be enormous. There were more than 2,300,000 gallons in the container when it burst, and I am certain that $500,000 would fall far short of reimbursement to the company alone.

"The disaster concerns us vitally and every effort is being made to determine exactly the cause, and who is concerned in it. The fluid was to be used in filling government contracts for alcohol for the manufacture of munitions. The firm has been filling war contracts almost since the war started, and before accepting contracts for the United States, it completed a number for the French and British governments.

W. L. Wedger, the state explosives expert, believed the explosion came from within the tank itself. He explained that the interior of the huge tank was lined with pipes for the purpose of heating the molasses so that it would flow freely into the tank cars in which it was transported to the plant in Cambridge. He stated that a mixture of gas and air "found vent in the blast."

The pier on which the tank was erected in 1916 was originally known as the Great White Spirit Wharf. Just before the disaster the huge structure had received several shipments of molasses, the last being a cargo from the American steamship *Milero*, which completed unloading 600,000 gallons from Matanzas on January 14.

When the *Milero* arrived, the weather was relatively cold, and there was minor difficulty when the colder molasses was discharged into the warmer supply already there.

A pumping station stood between the dock from which the ships discharged and the tank itself. Built as a subcellar with concrete walls and floor, the pumping station had machinery designed to suck the molasses through a 14-inch pipe from the ship through the room into the tank. As occasion demanded, the contents of the tank was transferred to freight cars especially built to carry the molasses along the street tracks of the Boston Elevated Railway to the distillery in Cambridge.

Before the tank was built in the vicinity of Copp's Hill, molasses had been unloaded at the wharf of the Boston Molasses Company in South Boston. Because of the long haul to Cambridge, it was decided to construct a tank on what by then had come to be known as Gas House Wharf. Rebuilt, the pier had served adequately until the disaster.

The United States Industrial Alcohol Company maintained only one employee at the tank wharf, William H. White of Sharon. He was in charge of the pumping station between the dock and the tank and was away at dinner when the disaster occurred.

Five of those killed worked in the city yards. Eating in a flimsy structure at lunchtime, they were engulfed when the explosion occurred and succumbed at once.

The devastated area presented such a fantastic spectacle that it drew enormous crowds. Onlookers gathered at many vantage points, including Copp's Hill Park, Commercial Street, and the lower part of Charter Street, and stared in awe at the scenes of utter ruin.

Thirty-three enlisted men from the U.S.S. *Pawnee*, which was lying close by the scene of the disaster, assisted in vital rescue work. Under the command of Ensign C. J. Campbell, they dug out several dead bodies from the molasses ooze near the elevated structure and managed to rescue five other persons still alive.

Directly under the overhanging girders of the elevated tracks they discovered the body of a woman of about seventy, so heavily smeared with molasses that she was believed dead until she spoke, asking for a priest. A priest soon came and called for an ambulance, and the woman was taken to the Relief Hospital. The sailors never discovered her name or whether she survived the ordeal.

A girl appealed to the sailor cadets from the training ship *Nantucket* for help. She told them she and a friend had been standing on Commercial Street in front of North End Park at the time of the blast. Her companion had been drawn toward the tank in a suction-like wind, while she found herself shot through the air away from the tank to land twenty feet from where she had been standing. Although the cadets dug in the debris where she thought the boy had been lost, he could not be found nor was his body ever discovered.

The work of the Women's Volunteer Relief Corps was praised by both the firemen and the police. Every available ambulance of the American Red Cross was sent to the scene, with Mary Converse in command of the ambulances at the disaster.

Firemen from Fireboat Engine 31 soon turned strong streams of water on the brown molasses fluid. The force proved fairly effective. Unfortunately, in places the molasses was so deep and clung in such a tenacious manner to the ground and the debris that an unbelievably long time was needed to wash the substance into the harbor.

Superintendent E. M. Byington of the Boston Fire Department Construction and Supplies Department was placed in charge of the almost impossible task of pumping out the cellars and basements in the area. Even after a week of work, several locations in the area were still deep in molasses. The worst hazard was a deep pool at the northern side of the Bay State freight house, a pool that stretched all the distance from Commercial Street to the cap-logs at the edge of the water-front.

Even with a number of Fire Department pumps working twenty-four hours every day, the drop in the level of the molasses was almost imperceptible. After days of pumping, the cellars of the freight house and other buildings in the area were still filled with molasses almost to the level of the first floor. The cellars of every store in the long brick block stretching from Copp's Hill Terrace to Charter Street on Commercial Street were still filled to the brim with molasses five days after the disaster.

Those who watched as the ruins were being cleared noticed with horror the number of horses that had been caught, still hitched to their wagons, when the explosion took place. Five of the unfortunate beasts of burden were pulled from the molasses in front of the remains of the freight shed of the Boston and Worcester Railway. As the debris was moved away, the five horses were discovered in a single heap. They had died rearing and struggling to free themselves from the awesome combination of wreckage and molasses.

It was just beyond the pile of horse carcasses that the remains of Henry Laird were found. He had been missing for several days. The body was on its side, the face turned outward. It was necessary to turn a stream from a fire hose on the body to clear away the congealed syrup for identification purposes. The dead man either had sought safety under the truck where he was discovered, or the flood of molasses had carried him there. His remains were still jammed under the truck when his head was uncovered, and powerful jacks were needed to lift the tons of debris from his body.

A total of thirteen persons were known to have lost their lives in the tank disaster.

After everything had been done for the living, the officials began asking each other why the tank had collapsed. Few of those engaged in supervising the clearing of debris agreed with the theory that the mere collapse of the tank could cause such havoc. It was the accepted decision of most of those examining the ruins that an explosion in the tank itself ripped the sides apart and gave the "avalanche of molasses the impetus which it manifested."

By Friday morning, January 17, the belief that an explosion had been responsible for the disaster had gained considerable strength. United States Inspector of Explosives Daniel F. O'Connell expressed the opinion that there was some evidence of fermentation, and stated that in many instances the holes in the tank were much larger than the rivets. The theory that the structure collapsed because of the fullness of the tank was not supported by O'Connell, although the huge molasses container was filled to capacity. Inspector O'Connell's report, which was forwarded to the Bureau of Mines in Washington, included an estimate that there had been 70 gallons of alcohol for every 100 gallons of molasses, presenting a condition of hazardous volatility.

Another factor considered was the beating upon the metal tank of the strong rays of the sun, which heated the structure. This, according to some, caused the liquid inside the tank to ferment and give off gas. The roof of the tank had four vent holes, but it was never made clear whether these vents allowed the escape of gas that might form inside. It was believed by those who worked at the tank that all four vents were either screwed down tight or had been jammed or gummed by molasses, thus preventing the escape of gas.

The evident force that crumpled the strong steel supports of the Elevated roadway was mentioned as reason to believe that an explosion of some sort must "have been the propulsion." Sections of the steel sides of the tank flew through the air to drop into Commercial Street itself.

Former Building Commissioner Patrick O'Hara stated positively that the disaster was the result of an explosion. He was familiar with the construction of the tank, and remarked that four years before he had inspected it carefully. He added that explosions of molasses were not unknown, and in this statement he had the backing of several chemists on the scene.

Chief John H. Plunkett of the Boston Fire Department stated that "the molasses in the tank had to be heated in order to keep it at a temperature which would allow it to be drawn easily from the tank. The heating was done by means of steam pipes run into the tank.

"In heating such tanks, great care must be used to prevent overheating. Molasses when fermenting, or when heated, throws off an alcoholic gas which has a tremendous pressure. Railroad authorities are always particular about providing vent for this gas when moving molasses.

"There is no regulation over the construction and use of such tanks. In my opinion there should be," the chief concluded.*

The task of delving through the wreckage took the full time of more than three hundred men from the Public Works Department, aided by a force from the Elevated railway and employees of the Hugh Nawn Contracting Company, for more than five weeks. There were thirty-five men cutting the fragments of the tank into movable pieces with acetylene torches, while the elimination of the molasses was a slow, painful job that kept the firemen constantly at their high pressure hoses.

It is said that never before in the history of the country did

* Because the tank was considered a receptacle and not a building, the municipal building department had absolutely no authority to supervise the construction of the tank. Commissioner Herbert A. Wilson introduced a new bill to give the municipal building authorities the power to regulate the construction of such structures in the future.

so many people file lawsuits for such a disaster. One scientist testified for three weeks, at times well into the night. It was not until 1926, six years after the disaster, that the molasses hearings came to a close.

Not only was it found that the tank itself had not been built strongly enough, but it came out in court that no real examination or inspection of the structure had ever been made! It was the conclusion of the experts that as the molasses weighed eleven pounds to the gallon, making a pressure of more than two tons per square foot on the sides and bottom of the container, the comparatively weak tank, never properly inspected, simply collapsed. Blame for the disaster was charged to the United States Industrial Alcohol Company, and the bill they eventually had to pay came to more than a million dollars.

As a result of the molasses disaster of 1919, more stringent regulations regarding the approval and inspection of similar tanks were enacted.

CHAPTER 3

THE PICKWICK CLUB COLLAPSE

Shortly before three o'clock in the morning of the Fourth of July 1925, an ominous cracking sound was heard by dancers at the Pickwick Club, located in the Old Dreyfus Hotel at 12 Beach Street in downtown Boston, a relatively short distance from the Atlantic Avenue waterfront and actually on the edge of Chinatown. Then the lights went out. For many of the more than one hundred and fifty merrymakers in the third-floor club it was a moment of terror that would end in death.

Band leader Billy Glennon and his trio of musicians were preparing for the "Good Night" number that would terminate the night's activities, but it was never played.

Sand and dust began to seep down from the ceiling, and then the entire floor collapsed. The ceiling of the club fell in, followed by both the fourth and fifth stories of the old hotel. Gigantic sections of the upper floors hung down, held together only by huge squares of tarpaper that still adhered to flooring and shattered walls.

In moments all available police and fire apparatus started for the scene of the disaster. Slowly, through the morning, order emerged from the chaos. A few hours after the collapse, under the glare of floodlights and flares, a systematic search through the ruins was in progress. By dawn thirteen bodies had been recovered. The total count would eventually reach forty-four victims.

Rescue Company One of the Boston Fire Department was an early arrival on the scene. Using an acetylene torch the fire fighters cut through the steel supports of the elevator cage. Then three trucks hooked onto the long elevator cables, and as a united effort was made, the cables began to stretch all the way across the street. Finally the cables and the cable drum toppled away from the top of the shaft. As they fell, a great cloud of dust, dirt, and even flames was seen. Hoses from the fire department soon extinguished the flames.

All day long screams were heard coming from several areas in the debris. At about ten in the evening the last cry was heard. Shortly before midnight a huge derrick lifted a section of the dance floor, revealing the remains of three more men and two women.

The legs and body of Mrs. Edith Jordan, a bride of a few weeks, were caught in the collapse, but she could talk to rescuers and did so for no less than eight and a half hours of effort. Finally liberated, she was rushed to the hospital but died before she could be removed from the ambulance.

The driver's license of Frank Jones of Beach Street in Wollaston, Massachusetts, was discovered in the ruins. His home was called and Frank Jones himself answered. Jones explained that he had lost his license in some manner two months before. He had no idea how the card turned up at the club, which he had not visited for several weeks.

As soon as the news of the Pickwick Club disaster became known, police lines were set on Washington Street and Harrison Avenue, just beyond the Beach Street debris. A bystander watching the grim spectacle described the crowds of onlookers.

"At the most, only a few hundred of them could see anything of the debris and the dust-covered, weary firemen and laborers engaged in digging for bodies. Except when the front wall crumbled to a pull from the fire department cables, there was nothing spectacular, nothing thrilling to see.

"Nonetheless, neither showers nor darkness routed them.

"If today had not been a holiday, the work of the police assigned to handling the crowds would have been more difficult. As it was, they had an opportunity to establish lines during the early morning hours when the district was almost deserted.

"Well before noon, however, the streets in the vicinity were crowded. Men and women appeared in windows and on roofs of buildings gazing on the sight. Eagerly snatching at rumors of faint cries heard down under the debris or of bodies being brought to the surface, the spectators waited, individuals changing now and then but the mass remaining the same tense, high-strung unit.

"Police officers commented on the fact that so many persons who took up their vigil at the ropes early in the day were still there when darkness fell.

" 'Some of them haven't eaten all day,' said one officer. 'They stand there, asking civilian officials and newspapermen who pass through the lines for information but never approaching an officer. Some of them must have friends or relatives who they think may have been in the place and yet they are too timid to go to the police.'

"Occasionally there would appear on the fringe of the crowd a man or more often, a girl, whose mission, it was obvious, was not to gratify morbid curiosity. Shyly, as if fearful of hearing the worst, as if preferring no news to definite information, she would accost officials or newspapermen leaving the scene.

" 'Do you know, mister, have they heard anything of so-and-so?' 'Have they taken out a girl in a blue dress, about twenty-two?' 'Maybe my chum is in there. Did you hear anything about—?'

"These questioners were probably not relatives of the persons of whom they sought word. More likely they were chums and pals, members of 'the gang,' who knew that their partners-in-play at times made merry at the nightclub.

"It never required long for rumors of such cries from the debris to reach the crowd. Invariably, as the word spread, there would issue from the watchers a mighty 'Hello-o-o, hello-o-o' that not even shouted calls for silence could suppress. It may have been a belief that their answer would be heard down in the depths of the debris that actuated the spectators; more likely, it was pent-up emotion bursting free. Crowds are ever hungry for a chance to cheer or yell—they had mighty little opportunity for either yesterday."

About two o'clock on that July Fourth afternoon jazz music could be heard playing in various Chinese restaurants in the vicinity. To the watchers below, the shadows of couples dancing made a strangely contrasting background for the gigantic piles of rubbish and debris from which the police were still taking dead bodies.

Rain began to fall shortly before sunset, and it was hoped that the dense crowds would thin out. Twenty minutes later a blanket-covered bundle on a stretcher was carried over to an ambulance, and those who were watching realized that bodies were still being found.

Half an hour after sunset myriads of lights that had been gathered together by the Edison Company were placed in position to give the most illumination possible. Fifty lights were put up along the distant side of the disaster, while twenty-five more were set up in buildings along Beach Street.

As darkness wore on, the watchers realized that their part in the grisly spectacle was similar to sitting in a gallery at a show—a terrible show, of course. They observed firefighters, police, officials, and laborers carrying out their duties in the midst of the giant lights, similar to actors on a spotlit stage.

The famous Gordon's Washington Street Olympia Theatre was temporarily closed. Two hundred early patrons were about to watch the show when the authorities decided to clear the theatre, for it was realized that one side wall of the theater ran along the ruins of the club. An actor announced that as rescuers were still searching for bodies a few feet away, it had been decided to stop the performance. There was no disorder as the patrons filed out, and it was explained to them that the measure was purely precautionary.

One story that aroused indignation was told by Harold Shaw, a waiter at the club. He declared that the side door of the premises was barred with a trick lock to prevent outsiders getting in. Shaw explained that the lock could be manipulated only by a member of the club who was familiar with the complicated mechanism.

At the time of the disaster Timothy Barry was president of the Pickwick Club and his brother was floor manager.

Almost every department of city and state was blamed for the disaster by those who lost loved ones in the collapse.

Investigations soon revealed that the Pickwick Club's walls actually had been weakened weeks before. Hugh Urquhart, an engineer who made a careful examination at the scene, revealed that on the Friday before the collapse he had been checking an elevator he had installed. Visiting 6 Beach Street, Urquhart had occasion to look at the exposed underpinnings of the Pickwick Club building, where he found seven four-foot piers with six-foot spaces between them. The clay under the piers had been removed, leaving them hanging alone with nothing to support them in any way!

District Attorney Thomas C. O'Brien was told that in excavating for a garage next door to the old hotel building, a steam shovel had been used. At the time an agreement had been made to protect and strengthen the hotel building. Actually, the lateral support had been removed, leaving the

Pickwick Club in a very dangerous state. However, even after half a century, there still are many opinions as to what type of structural weakness brought the building down.

Both Mayor James Michael Curley and Governor Alvin T. Fuller acted at once in representing the city and the commonwealth respectively. Mayor Curley made at least seven visits to the site in the next few days, while Governor Fuller appointed Attorney General Jay R. Benton to write a daily personal report to him on the investigation's progress.

At a grand jury assembled because of the disaster, testifying witnesses were called for visit after visit to the court so that the members of the jury could be crystal clear in their understanding of certain controversial points. Apparently determination of where to assign blame rested on interpretation of the General Laws. Although the Commonwealth of Massachusetts covers the situation in Chapter 143 of the General Laws, Boston is excepted from the general laws of the Commonwealth.

In the building laws for Boston, paragraph one, section three, the Boston Commissioner for Buildings is ordered to examine any edifice that has recently had a fire. On April 13 the building did have a fire, but although structural weakness was noted after the blaze, it was never repaired.

Many city residents and some officials claimed that the commonwealth was responsible for the collapse because a commonwealth-chartered group controlled the building. Secretary of the Commonwealth Frederick W. Cook emphatically and correctly stated that exclusive of the commonwealth, Boston had its own laws regarding buildings. "Any attempt to divert to the office of the secretary of state the responsibility for continued occupancy of an unsafe building, because it was supposed to be occupied by a chartered corporation is not only ridiculous but dastardly," concluded Cook.

Civil suits totaling more than a million dollars eventually were filed. Many of those interested in the political aspect of the situation wondered if the "higher-ups" would be made to answer for anything that contributed to the tragedy of July 4, 1925. There was a persistent rumor that some "higher-up" official had given the go-ahead for unrestricted revelry and dancing that July 4 eve in the weakened structure.

Those in the corridors outside the grand jury rooms were actually divided in their purposes. One group included lawyers interested in prospective clients, another those who desired to emphasize the civil liability aspect. It was also reported that one lawyer was bemoaning the fact that three of his clients, "all good pay," had died in the collapse.

Who was blamed after all the evidence was studied?

Governor Fuller's report included the statement that, without question, the premises would have been ordered vacated if a careful city inspection after the April 13 fire had been made. He also emphasized as a contributory factor the excavations made for the construction of a garage next door to the old hotel building, after which suitable and proper shoring had not been carried out.

General George Washington Goethals, who built the Panama Canal, made an inspection of the premises. He declared that the underlying cause of the building's collapse was the rotten condition of the concrete pilings.

The grand jury eventually indicted twelve men, including contractors, foremen, two city department officials, and several officials directly connected with the property or the Pickwick Club itself. The cause of the collapse was officially determined to be the failure of concrete piers under the building and the lack of lateral bracing. Nevertheless, all charges against those indicted were dropped.

Never before in Boston history had such a building disaster occurred. The panorama of the Pickwick Club collapse could not be forgotten by those who saw it.

PART TWO

From Massachusetts to Maine

~~~~~~~~~

CHAPTER 1

THE LAWRENCE MILL
DISASTER

Sailing up the Merrimack River from the Massachusetts coast, the adventuresome mariner eventually sights the buildings, steeples, and chimneys of Lawrence, which many have called Massachusetts' only "made city," as it was actually planned as a textile center.

When the clipper ship business of Boston was first affected by the progress of steamers, several shrewd capitalists and bankers of Massachusetts decided to seek other fields in which to make their investments. For the first time in the history of the state these industrial leaders planned to build and operate a city actually made to their own order. In 1845 they formed the Essex Company to utilize the power created by Bodwell's Falls in the Merrimack River near the area soon to be called Lawrence, Massachusetts, after Amos Lawrence, a prominent member of the group. Built almost overnight, Lawrence was incorporated as a town in 1847, and became a city six years later. As the years went by, other Bostonians became interested in the growing textile industry in this new city. Immigrants from Italy, Poland, Syria, Armenia, and Canada populated the area. The first mayor, elected in 1853, was Charles Storrow.

Four giant mills were soon completed, one of which—the Pemberton Mills—some said, was put up in much too rapid a fashion. It was asserted that it had been erected in a relatively flimsy manner. For example, in one case the wrong size horizontal beams for the upper stories had been furnished. The beams were too short and could not cross the vertical girders. Jury-rigged beams were substituted. In addition, several architects indicated that the walls of the mills were too thin, and they pointed out that unsatisfactory cast-iron pillars had been used in certain instances.

Nevertheless, all warnings and adverse comments were ignored. When it was announced that the great Pemberton Mills complex was finished, spindles and looms were moved in, and men, women, and children workers arrived. All went well for several years, and the objections were forgotten as month after month went by without incident or trouble.

Then came January 1860. On January 10, late in the afternoon, all the workers were busily engaged at their various occupations, keeping the spindles and looms functioning. The three turbine wheels, each yielding two hundred horsepower, were smoothly operating, and the boiler that heated the huge edifice, but housed in a separate building for safety, was operating perfectly. A line of hose ran from the pumps to every room in the mill.

Suddenly, at ten minutes before five, this vast, towering structure, 284 feet long and 84 feet wide, with most of the 650 looms and 29,000 spindles in operation, started to disintegrate.

One survivor, whose name does not come down to us, told his story later. He had been standing in the second-story carding room, where it was his task to light the burners. With no previous warning there was a fearful noise. As he stared spellbound the shafting ripped down from the ceiling, accompanied by a terrific noise from overhead.

He remained "nailed to the spot" in terror at such an unaccountable spectacle. He then heard the overseer shout for him to jump clear, but as he did so he was struck and knocked unconscious by the debris that hit him.

An instant later he recovered consciousness, finding himself buried in rubbish and debris so effectively that he nearly gave up hope of ever getting out alive. Nevertheless, dripping with blood, he shoved and pushed, forcing his way to the top of the rubble. As he did so, he climbed across the lifeless remains of a young girl. He pulled himself free and fought along a passageway that revealed two more mangled bodies. Finally he escaped from the ruins and the rubble.

A twenty-year-old girl also extricated herself from the ruins. She told how she had been working on the second floor at the time of the collapse. Suddenly, less than twenty feet away, she sighted portions of the building bulging inward. She began to run in the opposite direction but was caught by other crumbling walls in her path. She started for a side door, but it shattered into fragments as she approached it. Finally she fought her way to a window and was able to leap to the ground and flee from the collapsing structure.

Another woman survivor explained how she had been working on the third floor. Suddenly the entire ceiling above seemed to fall on her, and then she realized that her own floor was collapsing as well. As the building continued to disintegrate, she was caught by fragments of machinery. A heavy beam struck her head. She was held by the wreckage and was unable to move. Then pressure began to force her arms and legs away from her body in opposite directions, but a moment later another wall collapsed, and she felt herself freed. Squirming and wriggling, she fought her way out of the rubble and escaped.

An exploring party discovered a little girl. She lay apparently crushed beneath a gigantic iron block, her back pressed against a heavy timber and her left arm thrust to the elbow in a circular piece of metal. She was hopelessly wedged in the midst of heavy machinery. Four men tried to lift the iron girder but failed to budge it. A giant of a man who was unusually strong then attempted the task. Straining and groaning, he finally forced his body against the block and succeeded in lifting it a fraction of an inch. The others pulled the girl out. To their joy, the men found that the iron girder had been braced against another powerful obstruction in such a way that the girl, although tightly wedged, had been inside a protective metal shield around her body and actually was not seriously injured at all!

At one point in the rescue attempts a volunteer called for help in pulling on a rope attached to a projecting timber from under which cries had been heard. No one would help, for they feared the timber would come down on them. A woman then stepped out of the group. Standing by the single volunteer, she appealed to the others. Ashamed, several of the men also grabbed the rope. They pulled with a concerted effort and the timber slid out, revealing two victims still alive. They were rushed to the hospital.

Among the sufferers in the debris was an overseer who had been a favorite of the workers. As the search for victims went on, his voice was suddenly heard from the very depths of the ruins. Fighting down through the debris, the workers were almost to him when a fire broke out and pushed them back.

"Hurry," he cried, "I'll kill myself rather than burn to death!" Several minutes later they reached him, but he had cut his throat. Rushed to the hospital, he died of his self-inflicted injury on the way.

A large number of workers who had been in the weaving room on the lower floor had been able to crawl up on the debris of the second floor by going through a window that was still open. The heavy stone floor of the second story had not collapsed, and thus became a haven of safety, allowing many workers to save themselves there.

One forty-year-old woman had a miraculous escape. Working on the top floor, she had been precipitated headlong into the debris along with timbers, roofing, bricks, and machinery but managed to land on the bottom unharmed.

Walking along outside the building, a man heard the cry of a girl asking if Lizzie Hunt were still alive. The reply came from another section of the ruins that Lizzie was still unhurt. Both were later rescued and united.

In one section of the ruins the dead bodies of three girls were found, locked in each others arms. As the fire was then approaching, attempts were made to pull the remains out together, but this could not be done, and the bodies of all three were consumed by the fire.

In another section of the ruins a woman was dragged out, still alive. Her left arm had been torn from its socket, and her body and legs were terribly mangled. In spite of her injuries, she survived.

The dead body of a girl was discovered jammed between two giant girders, pressed in such a manner that the head was actually squeezed to the thickness of a hand. A woman nearby was rescued naked. Her clothing had been ripped completely off by the friction of debris and timbers.

Many heroic deeds were witnessed that terrible afternoon and evening. Little Mary Flint had shouted out for rescuers to save her friend Nash, who lay severely wounded near her. Mary's cry did help the rescuers to discover Nash's dead body. Nash's brother, caught alongside of him, died the moment he was uncovered. Poor Mary later succumbed to her own injuries.

Just before the flames started, a young girl was pulled to

safety. When questioned as to her condition, she replied that she was indeed all right, and "nothing is hurt." Actually, her right arm had been broken near the wrist. The excitement of her deliverance was so strong that she was totally unaware of her injury.

When the flames began, conditions soon became unbearable. The waterworks pipes connected to the mills had been broken when the building collapsed, and the presence of cotton waste saturated with oil made it almost impossible to put out the flames.

During the hours immediately following the building's collapse, the fire fighters of Lawrence and surrounding towns worked without relief. When the men were so exhausted that they could do no more, women volunteers spelled them, working the fire engines and doing their tasks well. Finally, at one o'clock the next morning, fire fighters won their battle and the conflagration was put out. Survivors and others saw nothing except a broad area of black smouldering ruins where 525 workers had been laboring the day before.

All New England, on hearing of the disaster, sent aid. The overwhelming need was to help children whose parents had perished. Brothers, sisters, and tiny babies had to be helped. Aged, infirm parents who had depended on their dead children were also in desperate need.

The city hall was converted into a hospital to shelter and bed the survivors. A desperate need for blankets, sheets, bandages, and medicine was announced, and eventually these arrived in Lawrence from many locations. Doctors and nurses worked throughout the night to aid the stricken. Many women who had never before attempted such tasks served as nurses in the emergency.

One man later stated that the spectacle he had witnessed had been "awesome, horrible, sickening, loathsome and shocking, all in one."

Sympathizing and curious thousands came to Lawrence from every part of New England. Each arriving train brought scores of visitors. Groups walked over to what was left of the Pemberton Mills and gazed at the rubble in wonder. It seemed an unbelievable disaster. Each day the bridge, the ice-bound canal, and the street that overlooked the debris of what had once been a six-story mill were thronged with living masses of humanity pressing as close to the ruins as the smoking remains would allow.

As the piles of debris gradually cooled, workers searched for additional bodies, applying themselves relentlessly to the gruesome task. On the morning after the disaster a cold, drizzling rain set in, which soon changed to snow.

Derricks were moved in to help in searching the ruins, and as the hours went by, more human remains were uncovered and transported to a so-called dead room nearby. Some bodies were found in almost perfect condition, similar to many remains found after the holocaust at the Cocoanut Grove in Boston more than eighty-two years later. Other bodies were so mutilated and disfigured that they could only be identified by the clothing they wore.

According to the jury brought together to assess blame, the disastrous calamity was caused by the imperfect and insufficient material used and the improper arrangement of that material in the construction of the building. The master mason in charge of the construction told the jury that "the walls were altogether too weak for such a structure." He testified that he had warned the mill owners, but his statements had been entirely disregarded. His warning went unheeded. The building eventually collapsed, bringing death to eighty-eight victims and misery to their relatives. Scores more suffered disfigurement and painful injury.

CHAPTER 2

AMERICA'S FIRST REVOLUTION

The Seal of the town of Ipswich, Massachusetts, declares that village to be "The Birthplace of American Independence." The story behind the inscription is interesting and important but relatively unknown beyond the Ipswich area. Dating the struggle for independence from 1775–76 is to ignore the first American revolution.

In the year 1686, the people of New England were enjoying virtual freedom from British control. The charter granted by King Charles I in 1630 was their only connection with England. They elected their own legislatures and chose their own officials. Later King Charles II felt that the New Englanders were getting out of hand and sent Edward Randolph to Boston as his special investigator. Randolph reported to the king that the colonists would not obey his commands, whereupon he was instructed to appoint commissioners with real power. Randolph's efforts were practically ignored. This so angered Charles that he ordered a *Quo Warranto* in the court of King's Bench, whereby the Massachusetts Bay Charter was rendered legally void. As of May 20, 1686, Massachusetts was without a charter.

During this so-called Inter-Charter period, Joseph Dudley

became president of the Massachusetts Provisional Government. Commissioned by the new monarch, King James II, Dudley governed from May 24, 1686, to the following December 20. He was succeeded by Sir Edmund Andros, a close friend of James II.

Andros arrived in Boston aboard the *Kingfisher*, Sunday, December 19, 1686, to take over the governorship of the disfranchised colonies. A staunch loyalist, the new governor was a gentleman of high connections and came from an important family. There are many who believe with historian John G. Palfrey that Andros had "a personal grudge against Massachusetts, on account of old affronts" and would be "as oppressive and offensive as the King desired." However, any governor sent to New England just after the people had lost their charter would be hated as the agent of a king they neither knew nor understood.

Sir Edmund Andros set up his government during the first half of 1687, appointing twenty-five councilors. In March he announced a repressive plan of taxation without representation and ordered every town in his domain to choose a local tax commissioner. The tax to be collected was twenty pence a head plus a penny a pound on the total valuation of each man's property.

Then he took another step that alienated him from many Bostonians. Belonging to the Church of England, he had no place to worship in Boston, that hotbed of Dissenters, and so demanded that the South Church be made available for him. Protests from church members merely brought a company of redcoats to protect the governor as he worshipped alone. The Bostonians, who were thus forced to wait in the streets for Andros' services to finish, were quite naturally resentful. This enforced triumph of the Church of England over the Dissenters was perhaps the first important step Andros took on his road to imprisonment.

A meeting of great importance to New Englanders took place in the town of Ipswich, Massachusetts, on August 23, 1687—a protest against Andros' action in ordering the appointment of a local commissioner to prepare tax lists.

The citizens of Ipswich went on record as being ready to rebel against the representative of the King of England in his demand for the appointment of a tax commissioner. They refused to appoint the commissioner, claiming that "the sd act doth infringe their Liberty as Free Borne English subjects of his Majesties by interfering with ye statutory Laws of the Land."

Needless to say, Governor Andros did not agree with this statement by the Ipswich town meeting and sent his soldiers to arrest the six most active members: John Andrews, chairman of the selectmen and moderator of the meeting; John Appleton, town clerk; William Goodhue; Robert Kinsman; Thomas French; and the Reverend John Wise. They were brought back to Boston and imprisoned.

On October 3, 1687, after twenty-one days in jail, the six defendants were brought to trial in Boston. The entire colony seethed with excitement and expectation. Judge Joseph Dudley announced what he believed was the brutal truth, that "the people in New England were all slaves . . . and that they must not think the privileges of Englishmen would follow them to the end of the world." The prisoners were convicted and fined from fifteen to fifty pounds each; in addition they were to share costs amounting to four hundred pounds. The Reverend Mr. Wise was forbidden to preach and the others were not allowed to hold office.

Andros had gained a temporary victory. Every town in Massachusetts now fell in line and appointed tax commissioners. But it became known that Judge Dudley had called the New Englanders slaves, and his statement rankled deep in the hearts of the liberty-loving people of Massachusetts. The citizens of Boston and the surrounding countryside held secret meetings and discussions that were to lead to important developments within the next few weeks. When Sir Edmund Andros returned to Boston in March 1689 after a campaign to what is now Maine, he noticed a change in the people's attitude that approached open hostility. Andros' soldiers began deserting by the score, forming small independent bands.

It became noised about that Governor Andros "intended nothing but RUINE TO THEM," and the town of Boston was soon in great turmoil. Local leaders met and agreed that unless they acted quickly, the discharged soldiers and others would start "a great stir and produce a bloody Revolution," as Cotton Mather's son admitted later. They appointed a delegate, probably Cotton Mather, to prepare a Declaration of Independence, indicating that they expected the worst and, secretly, may have hoped for it.

On April 16, 1689, Andros mentioned in a letter that a "general buzzing among the people" was quite noticeable. But it was not until April 18, at eight in the morning, that "it was reported . . . that at the north end they were all in arms." Captain John George of the British frigate *Rose* was seized and at nine o'clock drums were beaten throughout the town as if by prearranged signal. The insurrectionists descended upon the leading lieutenants of Governor Andros. They captured William Sherlock, Ravenscroft, White, George Foxcroft, Edward Randolph, Broadbent, and Crafford and hurried them off to prison. When the keeper objected, he, too, was thrust into prison, and Scates, a bricklayer, became the new jailer.

There was a mighty demand for the aged Simon Bradstreet, governor at the time the charter was withdrawn and now nearly ninety years old, to take over the reins of government. The insurrectionists escorted Bradstreet and several others to the Town House. As they looked down upon the milling crowd gathered in the street, Bradstreet and his friends heard themselves acclaimed as the only persons qualified to establish the new government. The new executives then gathered at the Town House and nervously read over their previously prepared Declaration.

This first American Declaration of Independence is indeed a notable document, surprisingly similar in spirit to the Declaration of 1776. I quote from the more interesting and important parts of the lengthy text:

THE DECLARATION OF THE Gentlemen, Merchants, and Inhabitants of *Boston*, and the Country Adjacent, April 18, 1689.

We have seen more than a decade of Years rolled away, since the *English* World had the Discovery of an horrid . . . Plot . . . to Crush and break a Country . . . entirely.

To get us within the reach of the desolation desired for us . . . we . . . first have our Charter Vacated . . . before it was possible for us to appear at Westminster. . . .

We were put under a *President and Council* without any liberty for an Assembly . . . by a Commission from his *Majesty*. . . . The Commission was as *Illegal* for the form of it, as the way of obtaining it was *Malicious* and *unreasonable*. . . . Yet we made no Resistance thereunto . . . because we took pains to make ourselves believe as much as ever we could of the Whedle then offer'd unto us. . . .

In little more than half a year we saw this Commission superseded by another, yet more Absolute and Arbitrary, with which Sir *Edmund Andros* arrived as our Governor: who . . . planned to make Laws and raise Taxes as he pleased. . . . We were chiefly *squeez'd* by a crew of abject Persons, fetched from *New York* . . . by these were extraordinary and intollerable Fees extorted from everyone upon all occasions. . . .

It was now plainly affirmed . . . that the people in *New England* were all *Slaves*. . . . Accordingly we have been treated with multiplied contradictions to *Magna Charta,* the rights of which we laid claim to.

Persons who did but peacefully object against the raising of Taxes without an Assembly, have been for it fined, some twenty, some thirty, and others fifty Pounds. . . . Packt and pickt Juries have been very common things. . . . Without a *verdict*, yea, without a Jury sometimes have People been fined most unrighteously, and some . . . have been kept in long and close Imprisonment without . . . *Habeas Corpus* allowed unto them. . . .

Writs of Intrusion began everywhere to be served on People. . . . We do therefore seize upon the Persons of those few *Ill men* which have been (next to our Sins) the grand Authors of our Miseries. . . . In the meantime . . . we commit our Enterprise unto Him *who hears the cry of the Oppressed.*

The contributors to this Declaration of Independence then composed a letter to Sir Edmund Andros, telling him that the people had taken arms and seized the town. They said that for the purpose of "quieting and securing . . . the People from . . . emminent Dangers . . . We judge it necessary you forthwith surrender and deliver up the Government and Fortification. . . . Otherwise we are assured they will endeavor the taking of the Fortification by Storm, if any Opposition be made." The letter was signed by the fifteen leaders in the Town House, including Simon Bradstreet, John Nelson, William Stoughton, and Waite Winthrop.

Sir Edmund Andros was barricaded in at the defenses on

Fort Hill when the letter from the revolutionists reached him. Andros was sooned joined by Joseph Dudley and Colonel (Charles) Lidget. The governor asked Dudley if he would go out to the homes of the ministers of Boston and request them to appear at the fort, where possibly they could quiet the people. But Dudley told Andros that he would be captured the moment he left the fort, and the plan was abandoned.

At the Town House when the venerable Simon Bradstreet went out on the balcony to accept the cheers of the multitudes, as I mentioned above, his act probably prevented bloodshed, as historian Samuel G. Drake wrote in 1856. Colors were run up on Beacon Hill as a signal to the thousands on the Charlestown side that the moment for action was at hand. In the harbor the British frigate *Rose* opened her gunports and hoisted her battle flags. However, Captain Winthrop sent a note out to the lieutenant in command of the frigate saying that if the *Rose* fired a single shot into the town, her master, Captain John George, who had been captured by the revolutionists, would be executed. This bold note accomplished its purpose. Though the lieutenant commanding the *Rose* pretended he would soon fire, he never did, and finally accepted defeat and sent in his sails as a token of surrender.

But the excitement was not yet ended. Watching his chances, Governor Andros signaled for a boat to approach from the frigate and went down on the Battery Wharf with ten of his associates. The unruly mob outguessed the group, however, and captured the boat as it landed at the wharf. In the boat were hand grenades, small arms, and "a quantity of match!" Governor Andros and his party hurried back to the fort when they saw their scheme had miscarried.

A battalion of soldiers led by John Nelson of Long Island, Boston Harbor, then appeared at the fort and ordered Governor Andros to surrender. For a moment it looked as though the guns of the fort would be fired into the unruly crowd of soldiers and civilians, but after due consideration Sir Edmund decided that surrender was his best move. It had been a bloodless revolution.

After his acknowledgment of defeat, Andros was taken to the Town House, where Mr. Bradstreet waited to receive him. William Stoughton was the first to speak. He told the governor in no uncertain terms that he had only himself to blame for "the disaster" that had befallen him. Andros was confined for the night in Mr. John Usher's house and the next day taken to Fort Hill and imprisoned. Later he was incarcerated at Castle Island, from which he made two unsuccessful attempts to escape. His first escape attempt was foiled when an alert guard noticed military boots showing under the woman's clothing Andros was wearing as disguise. The second time he got as far as Rhode Island before being apprehended.

Happily for the people of New England, affairs in England were also reaching a state of crisis. A new king, William of Orange, was brought over from the Continent to take the throne away from James II. Increase Mather, who had fled from Boston to England, obtained audience with the new king and interceded as best he could on behalf of the New Englanders. On July 4, 1689, exactly eighty-seven years before the Declaration of Independence was drawn up in Philadelphia, King William told Increase Mather that he would approve the results of the American Revolution of 1689, without, however, renewing the old charter. The following month the king sent a Royal Letter ratifying the government of New England, but actually the colonists did not receive all the liberties for which they asked.

Stuart opposition to William of Orange was still strong in England and did not collapse until the Battle of the Boyne on July 1, 1690. But with the defeat of the Stuart supporters, there was no more danger to the New Englanders from across the sea. They would not be punished for their revolution in

New England, for in England the same thing had happened, and they would be allowed many of the things for which they had rebelled.

It was not until the 1760's that England and New England were once again in conflict, and then the difficulties could not be resolved without a great war. Whether or not the accession to the English throne by William of Orange prevented this country from realizing her independence in 1689 rather than 1775 is a question that offers an interesting subject for debate.

~~~~~~~~

CHAPTER 3

MOLL PITCHER

Thirty years ago, when Alton Hall Blackington took me to the site of the famed Moll Pitcher's home on the North Shore of Massachusetts, I was impressed by the atmosphere that seemed to pervade the area, even though Moll Pitcher had been dead for generations. Blackington, who was always meticulous in his research and writings, explained to me the deep hold this seer of a former century had everywhere in New England.

Samuel Adams Drake was the first writer of the modern era to tell us of the accomplishments of Moll Pitcher. In his book on New England legends, Drake explains that

[the city of Lynn] is likely to be celebrated throughout all time as having been the residence of the most successful fortune-teller of her day and generation—we might also say of whom we have any account in mystical lore, ancient or modern. While she lived she was without a rival in her peculiar art, and the prophetic words that she let fall were capable of being transmuted into gold.

It was once said of Napoleon that he left a family, but no successor. Moll Pitcher left no one her wonderful gift of foretelling the future by practising palmistry, or by simply gazing into the bottom of a teacup. . . . Yet even the most incredulous were compelled to admit her predictions to be wholly unaccountable; while those who came to laugh went away vanquished, if not fully convinced.

What is singular is that her reputation has rather increased than diminished with time. We have no account of her dupes, nor is there any "Exposure" extant.*

Moll Pitcher dwelt at the foot of High Rock, a remarkable cliff of dull red porphyry, which stands high over Lynn as the Citadel does over Quebec. During the fifty years that she pursued her trade of fortune-telling she was known all over New England for her successful predictions, some of which occurred ten and even twenty years after she had foretold them. She was a woman of shrewdness, penetration, and wit, and the residents of Lynn accepted her claim to foreknowledge because of the unequivocal testimony of the many hundreds who could attest to the accuracy of her predictions.

According to reports of the period, Moll was not the decrepit, withered, and toothless crone of Spenser, or Otways' "wrinkled hag, with age grown double,/Picking dry sticks and mumbling to herself." In the prime of her life Moll was a woman of medium stature, with an unusually large head, dark brown hair, and a thin, pale, and rather intellectual face. Her countenance was clouded with habitual sadness, indicating a mind burdened with the confidences, even the crimes, of the hundreds of individuals who sought her advice. She had a full forehead, arched eyebrows, eyes that seemed to read the secret thoughts of those who approached her, a nose "inclined to be long," and thin lips, but her visage had none of the wildness of the traditional witch of legend and lore.

* Samuel Adams Drake, *New England Legends*, pages 137–148.

During her active years, when she lived in a lonely and little frequented section of Lynn, Moll was consulted not only by the poor and ignorant, but by the rich and educated as well. Her most valued clients came from the wealthy seaports of the area. Common sailors and sea captains, cabin boys and the owners of ships, all visited her humble abode to learn the luck of coming voyages. It is even claimed that vessels were deserted on the eve of sailing because of Moll's predictions of doom.

Her advice was also much sought by treasure seekers, a rather numerous class in her day. To them Moll would reply, "Fools! If I knew where money was buried, do you think I would part with the secret?"

Moll Pitcher, born in 1738, was originally from Marblehead and is said to have inherited the gift of prophecy from her grandfather, John Dimond, who had the reputation there of being a wizard. Whenever a violent gale at sea arose, Dimond would go to the old burying ground on the hill, and there in the midst of the darkness and the storm, he would direct vessels then at sea, instructing them on how to weather the gale. Pacing up and down among the gravestones, in a voice that could be heard even above the howling of the tempest, he would shout his orders to the helmsman or the crew, just as if he were actually on the quarter-deck of the craft. Although astounded and terrified by his behavior, very few of the simple fisherfolk of Marblehead doubted his ability to bring ships safely into port.

Moll Pitcher's father was master of a small vessel and was not noted for wizardry of any type. In 1760 Moll, whose proper name was Mary Dimond, married Robert Pitcher, a shoemaker. She lived until 1813 when she was seventy-five. According to Lynn historian Alonzo Lewis, who remembered her, Moll was related to some of the best families in Essex.

He states that, except for her fortune-telling pretension, there was nothing disreputable in her life, and that her descendants were living and respected when he wrote.

Such is the picture of the celebrated fortune teller that has come down to us from her contemporaries. However, American literature presents quite a different portrait, drawn in verse.

In the year 1832 John Greenleaf Whittier published, anonymously, a poem in which Moll Pitcher is presented less than favorably. In an unusual opening statement to the poem, Whittier says:

> I have not enough of the poetical mania in my disposition
> to dream of converting, by an alchemy more potent than
> that of the old philosophers, a limping couplet into a
> brace of doubloons, or a rickety stanza into a note of
> hand. Moll Pitcher (there's music in the name) is the off-
> spring of a few weeks of such leisure as is afforded by
> indisposition, and is given to the world in all its original
> negligence—the thoughts fresh as when first originated.

Whittier's poem is the story of a maiden, fond and fair, whose sailor lover has gone on a long voyage to sea, where "He sought for gold—for yellow gold," in order to return a rich man and marry the girl waiting at home for him. While he is away, the maiden's mind becomes filled with gloomy forebodings concerning her lover. Obeying an uncontrollable impulse, she seeks the well-trodden path leading to Moll Pitcher's abode, in order to learn her destiny. While on her way to the house, she encounters Moll, who is thus described:

> She stood upon a bare tall crag
>   Which overlooked her rugged cot—
> A wasted, gray, and meagre hag,
>   In features evil as her lot.

She had the crooked nose of a witch,
   And a crooked back and chin;
And in her gait she had a hitch,
And in her hand she carried a switch,
   To aid her work of sin,—
A twig of wizard hazel, which
Had grown beside a haunted ditch,
Where a mother her nameless babe had thrown
To the running water and merciless stone.

The fortune teller has a secret enmity towards her trembling
visitor and wickedly determines to bring evil on the girl. Moll
leading the way,

   The twain passed in—a low dark room,
      With here and there a crazy chair,
   A broken glass—a dusty loom—
   A spinning-wheel—a birchen broom,
      The witch's courier of the air,
   As potent as that steed of wings
      On which the Meccan prophet rode
   Above the wreck of meaner things
      Unto the Houris' bright abode.
   A low dull fire by flashes shone
   Across the gray and cold hearthstone,
   Flinging at times a trembling glare
   On the low roof and timbers bare.

In these mysterious surroundings, the weird woman proceeds
to try her art by looking into the sorceress's cup. Presently she
speaks.

   Out spoke the witch,—'I know full well
      Why thou hast sought my humble cot!

Come, sit thee down,—the tale I tell
    May not be soon forgot.'
She threw her pale blue cloak aside,
    And stirred the whitening embers up,
And long and curiously she eyed
    The figures of her mystic cup;
And low she muttered while the light
Gave to her lips a ghastlier white,
And her sunk eyes' unearthly glaring
Seemed like the taper's latest flaring:
'Dark hair—eyes black—a goodly form—
    A maiden weeping—wild dark sea—
A tall ship tossing in the storm—
    A black wreck floating—*where is he?*
Give me thy hand—how soft, and warm,
    And fair its tapering fingers seem!—
And who that sees it now would dream
That winter's snow would seem less chill
Ere long than these soft fingers will?
A lovely palm!—how delicate
    Its veined and wandering lines are drawn!
Yet each are prophets of thy fate—
    Ha!—this is sure a fearful one!
That sudden cross—that blank beneath—
    What may these evil signs betoken?
Passion and sorrow, fear and death—
    A human spirit crushed and broken!
Oh, thine hath been a pleasant dream,
But darker shall its waking seem!'

Overcome by the terrible prophecy, to which her own fears give ready belief, the poor girl loses her senses. She is always watching for the sail in the offing, but it does not come. Wandering up and down the rocky shores of Nahant, she gazes vacantly out to sea. Then one day, in spite of Moll's fatal prediction, the lover's ship sails into the bay, and with it the one thing capable of restoring the maiden's reason again.

The witch, however, does not escape the consequences of her malevolence. She dies miserably in her wretched hovel, cared for in her last moments by a little child of the woman she has so cruelly wronged.

I prefer the real story of Moll Pitcher to that of the poet Whittier.

CHAPTER 4

FANNY CAMPBELL,
WHO LOVED AND WON

No less than twenty female pirates have been mentioned in the various books I have written. Among them were Madame Ching and Mrs. Lo, who operated pirate fleets after their husbands' deaths, and Madame Wong, who began her career without help from the other sex. The Pennsylvania-born pirate Rachel Wall, who married the man of her choice at Long Wharf in Boston, was mentioned in a broadside, but we do not know why she became a pirate. Ann Bonney and Mary Read became pirates for the sheer adventure of it. Mrs. Edward Jordan became a renegade in 1809 when she and her husband stole a ship. The Danish woman outlaw Alwida became a pirate to avoid marriage but eventually married the very person whose attentions made her take up piracy in the first place. Maria Cobham was a female fiend who relished her murderous avocation.

Fanny Campbell, the subject of this chapter, turned pirate for one single, unselfish motive.

In 1917 John Austin Belden of Wareham, Massachusetts,

was suffering from the grippe. Visited by Dr. Charles Edward Lovell, a relative of his, he began talking about ancestors in general. Growing more and more personal, Belden finally reached a point in the discussion where the doctor held up his hand.

"Now, John," he began, "this is all well and good, but I advise you to be careful about asking me to tell you too many things concerning our ancestors. You know, I am in possession of knowledge which you might not wish to discover."

"What do you mean by that?"

"Well, it's this way, John. If I tell you what I know, you may always be sorry I spoke up; and if I don't tell you, then everything will be as it was before. Would you like to know all about your ancestors? If not, the knowledge will die with me. Which way do you want it?"

"I'd like to know, Charles, especially now that you've got my curiosity aroused. You might as well tell me what you're hinting at and get it over with. Come on, Charles; let's have it."

And so it was that Dr. Lovell revealed to his astonished relative that one of his ancestors had turned pirate more than a hundred years earlier and had never been apprehended. Dr. Lovell explained that the entire carefully written story was in his possession, and if John Belden wished it, Dr. Lovell would will the material to him.

In October 1930 Dr. Lovell died, and Mr. Belden came to possess the precious document with its startling revelation. The day he acquired the information Belden took it upstairs into his room. There he opened the sealed envelope, which contained the strange history of his own great-great-grandmother, together with a drawing of her in color. He stayed in his room that night until he had learned all the remarkable facts of his ancestor's life. Her story follows:

In the year 1773, two fishermen, Henry Campbell and

Richard Lovell, lived side by side at the base of High Rock, Lynn, Massachusetts. Campbell's daughter, Fanny, and Lovell's son, William, had grown up with each other and fallen in love. William was then nineteen and Fanny a year younger.

William Lovell, who had sailed and fished in Boston Bay from the time he could walk, was anxious to become a deep-sea sailor and received permission from his parents to take a voyage from Boston. Six months later he returned, tanned and mature, and Fanny was very pleased with the change in her young friend. William told her about the foreign lands he had visited, and she in turn expressed a desire to make an ocean voyage herself.

Then came the eve of his second sailing, and the two climbed to the top of High Rock, where they talked of the future. Fanny was an active girl. She rowed a boat, shot panthers in the nearby Lynn Woods, rode a horse, and could handle a sailboat with the best of men. William confided to her that he would leave the sea if she so desired, but she told him to go ahead and work his way up until he was captain of his own vessel. At the conclusion of their talk they returned home.

William Lovell arose early the next morning and sailed away aboard the ship *Royal Kent*.

Meanwhile, at the Campbell residence, Fanny had another caller, a young man William had never met. His name was Captain Robert Burnet, and he was an officer in the British navy. Captain Burnet at first was but casually interested in Fanny, however later his attentions turned to love.

While at sea, William thought frequently of the girl back in Lynn and determined to ask her hand in marriage on his return. But before this could be, a day's sail from Port au Plate, a suspicious-looking schooner appeared on the horizon and gave chase.

As the stranger closed the distance between the two vessels, she displayed a skull and crossbones from her forepeak. The captain of the *Royal Kent* ordered all hands to prepare the cannons for defense, and soon the ship was firing at the pirate craft. The six-pounders caused devastating damage to the sea ruffians, but still they came nearer and nearer. Finally the pirates overtook the *Royal Kent*, threw grapnels across to the ship, and boarded her. Fighting their way along the deck, the marine bandits soon overwhelmed the American sailors, whom they outnumbered four to one. In the skirmish the *Royal Kent*'s captain killed the pirate chieftain and in turn was run through by the sword of another pirate. In all, the American sailors killed more than twice the number they lost, but this worked against them afterward. With their numbers diminished, the pirates forced the Americans to join their ranks. The *Royal Kent* was then scuttled.

The pirates went ashore at Tortuga, each man burying his own share of the treasure taken from the *Royal Kent*. No one knew where his fellow pirate had buried his loot; and if a man happened to be killed, it was only by chance that this treasure was ever recovered.

The pirates soon went to sea again. Seriously wounded in the engagement, Lovell was allowed to recover before he was ordered to take an active part in sailing the pirate craft. One night the ship was practically becalmed close to the shores of Cuba. Lovell and two companions, Jack Herbert and Henry Breed, were chosen for the same watch. Together they decided to make an attempt for freedom before morning. The three New Englanders were in full charge of the vessel during the graveyard watch. A light wind had sprung up, and when the moment for action came, they headed the schooner into it, lashed the wheel amidships, and silently let a small boat over the side. With great caution they put a few provisions aboard the boat and then scrambled down the rope ladder. Keeping an eye on the schooner, they rowed desperately for the shore half a mile away, and when the breeze freshened they hoisted sail and set a course for Havana.

After many hardships they reached the Cuban capital, elated at their success in escaping the pirates. Before they could find friends, however, the three Americans were arrested on suspicion of being pirates themselves. Technically they had been pirates ever since they were put aboard the outlaw schooner, and they had no proof that they had been forced to join the buccaneers.* Thrown into jail before they could get help, they waited week after week for their trial. Six months went by before they were brought to the advocate for their appearance in court. When no evidence was brought forward against them, the judge ordered them returned to their cells. Their despair was complete.

Back in Massachusetts, Fanny Campbell waited anxiously with no word from her lover. Months went by. Captain Burnet's visits to her home became more and more frequent, but Fanny remained true to her sailor sweetheart.

In Havana, the three Americans watched the months pass, but no one came to release them. Finally, two years after they had been imprisoned, William's friend, Jack Herbert, escaped from the jail. After making his way to an American ship then at the pier in Havana, he told his story and received permission to hide aboard until the vessel was due to sail. Then he was allowed to travel back to Boston on the ship. Bearing a letter to Fanny from William, he visited the girl shortly after landing. His unexpected call made her very happy. She questioned him about the great bastille in which William and young Breed were still incarcerated, and he explained how the guards

---

* Under similar conditions, to escape the possible charge of piracy, other suspected pirates brought the infamous John Phillip's head to Boston in a pickle barrel as evidence. See my *Pirates and Buccaneers of the Atlantic Coast*, p. 123.

were placed around the prison in such numbers that it was practically hopeless to attempt an escape.

When it was time for Herbert to return home, Fanny obtained his address—the foot of Copp's Hill in Boston. As he left, she mysteriously told him to make himself ready at a moment's notice for a strange adventure she was planning, an event that might take place at any time, day or night, in the near future. Although he was bewildered by her secretive manner, Jack Herbert agreed, and as he traveled by stagecoach from Lynn to Boston his mind dwelt on Fanny Campbell and her plans.

Captain Burnet called on Fanny the following evening and learned that William was still alive. Burnet had never considered William a real obstacle to his intentions, believing the lad merely a childhood sweetheart who would soon be forgotten. Fanny, however, convinced Burnet that night that she loved William alone, and in his disappointment the captain left her home earlier than he had planned, chagrined at the turn events had taken.

At Copp's Hill in Boston, Jack Herbert awaited developments. A week after his visit to Fanny's home, a man dressed as a common sailor knocked at his door and reminded him of his promise to be ready for a strange adventure. The visitor explained the situation carefully and got Herbert's agreement to sail on the brig *Constance*, a new sailing vessel soon to start a voyage to Cuba.

The following night Herbert went aboard the brig to find her well armed. The captain, Brownless by name, was a tyrant; the first mate, Banning, an imbecile; but the second officer, an unusual character named Channing, was a good sailor and well liked by the Americans in the crew.

As it happened, the captain was planning to proceed to England by way of Cuba. Once in England the entire crew would be pressed into the British navy for a term of three years. Channing already knew of the captain's scheme and had decided to use it to his own advantage.

Early one day when the *Constance* had reached the warmer waters of the West Indies and the brig was less than two days' sail from Cuba, Channing went down into the captain's cabin and found the master just getting up. Stepping to the captain's table, he seized a brace of pistols there and took a cutlass down from the bulkhead. Then Channing confronted the master.

"Captain Brownless, you are my prisoner!"

"Sir?"

"You are my prisoner!"

"Mutiny?"

"If you wish, but resistance is futile. If you attempt to leave the cabin you are a dead man."

Realizing his weapons were gone, Captain Brownless agreed to surrender. Channing tied up the captain and locked him in his cabin. Going to the quarters of the first mate, he explained what had happened.

"Why, that's piracy!" shouted Banning.

"Yes," answered Channing, "you are right."

Banning looked up at the young man and noticed his determined countenance. "How about me? Will you spare my life?"

"There's no danger at present if you remain quiet."

Channing then tied Banning up and locked him in his quarters, after which he went to Jack Herbert, who had the helm.

"Call the crew aft, Jack," he ordered. Ten minutes later, with the crew assembled on the deck, Channing explained that he had taken over the ship. Although there was some grumbling, shouts of delight came from every American present when it was learned that Captain Brownless had planned to impress them into the British navy as soon as they reached England. They agreed to accept Channing as their new captain.

The cook, a British subject, had other ideas and decided to

kill Channing and take the ship back as soon as he had the opportunity. Strangely enough, Captain Brownless had worked
out a similar plan, having made arrangements with the brig's
jailer to escape. The following night, independent of each
other, the two men started for Channing's quarters. Meeting in
the darkness outside the second mate's door, they fought and
fatally wounded each other, each thinking he had engaged in
combat with Channing.

A crew member came across the bodies and aroused Channing at once. The pirate captain was horrified at what had
occurred. At noon the following day he gathered the sailors
together for a burial service at sea. After Channing read a
portion of the Bible, the remains of the two men were slid
overboard into the sea and the voyage continued.

Several days later the *Constance* sighted a British bark, the
George out of Bristol. Confident of the firepower of his six
carronades, the *George*'s captain decided to engage in battle
with what he suspected was a pirate craft, but after a short
exchange with cannon, the Britishers realized they were losing
the engagement and surrendered. They were soon secured below deck on the bark, command of which was given to Jack
Herbert.

The two vessels sailed along side by side for a few days,
when suddenly mutiny broke out aboard the *George*. Channing
watched from the other craft as Herbert was roped and thrown
to the deck. He crossed over to the *George* at once in a small
boat. Going aboard with drawn pistols, he put down the mutiny, but was forced to kill one of the mutineers.

Finally the ships reached the desired point off the Cuban
shore near where William Lovell was a prisoner. Channing
ordered Jack Herbert to pick eight loyal members of his crew
and tell them all about the fort where his two former comrades
were imprisoned. Late that night the nine conspirators left the
vessel in a small boat and rowed for the fort. When they

reached land, the sailors put one man on the beach to guard their boat. The others crept silently toward the nearest sentry. Jumping on the unfortunate Spaniard, they quickly overcame him. They took care of the next guard in a similar way. Two more soldiers, representing the entire complement of sentries then remaining on duty, were surrounded and tied up, after which the four victims, still relatively unharmed, were carried into the guardhouse and locked away for the night.

Armed with the keys, Herbert stealthily walked with his associates into the subterranean passageway that led to the cell. Quietly unlocking the door, he found Breed and Lovell, awakened them, and led them out of the prison. An hour later all eleven Americans were in the boat, rowing desperately for the brig. Their luck had been good, but it couldn't possibly last much longer. Sure enough, just as they pulled up to the side of the *George,* they all heard the distant, unmistakable roll of the fort drums. The citadel was being aroused, for their daring feat had been discovered.

The anchors were weighed and the sails set. The two vessels were soon a substantial distance offshore and, as it turned out, all danger from the Spaniards was over.

Captain Channing, whose greeting to William Lovell was reserved but friendly, appointed him first mate of the *Constance.* Several days later the captain called Lovell down into the cabin and there revealed to the startled mate that he, Captain Channing, was in reality Fanny Campbell. She had dyed her face brown, cut her hair short, and donned a marine officer's uniform to complete the disguise. Needless to say, the pair had a happy reunion, but Fanny cautioned William against letting the others know.

For the next few days the *Constance* and the *George* continued their voyage uneventfully, but then they fought and captured a British merchantman. From this ship they learned that the British and Americans were engaged in a formal war, the Revolution. Realizing that her two craft could become privateers and escape the stigma of piracy, Fanny called the crews together and explained the situation. All but four men who were British agreed to become privateers. Of course it was not in order, but Fanny declared that formal application for privateer status would be made the moment they reached Massachusetts.

The next day a British armed sloop appeared and was quickly overcome by the two American craft. The discovery that Captain Burnet, who had sought Fanny's hand, was an officer aboard the sloop was quite a shock to both Fanny and William, but Burnet was shackled below with the other prisoners. Although Captain Burnet recognized Fanny, he did not tell the Americans that their captain was a woman, and they never did find out.

Fanny heard from the prisoners that Boston was occupied by the British, so she set course for Marblehead. It was in that harbor a week later that her two craft were made legal privateers of the new nation.

The next day Fanny and William reached High Rock, Lynn, and made their presence known to their happy families. The two lovers announced that their marriage would take place the very next week. After their wedding, William reluctantly went back to sea as captain of one of the privateers. His friend, Jack Herbert, was master of the other.

William served his country until the war came to an end, after which he made several long trips to China and then retired from the sea. By that time the family of William and Fanny Lovell was a large one. When their sons and daughters grew up and were married, the fact that Fanny had been a pirate at one time was kept secret. Their descendants are many and, as I have already mentioned, include John Austin Belden of Wareham.

CHAPTER 5

~~~~~~~~~

NANCY'S BROOK

Dino Valz was the first person to take me around the White Mountains. Dr. Robert Moody of Boston University introduced the two of us in 1934 when I was struggling with my first book. Dino had climbed the famed Matterhorn, and when he suggested doing the Presidential Range, Mrs. Snow and I accepted the challenge and went with him. I'll always remember his motto—"just one more hill." After what seemed like a hike of a hundred miles we all spent the night in the Lake of the Clouds hut, actually a substantial building. There was an overflow of visitors, and at least two dozen couples slept on the tables, arranged side by side in one long row.

Dino was the first person to tell me about Nancy and Nancy's Brook. Since then I've done a tremendous amount of research. The beginnings of the story were written more than a century ago by Anna C. Swasey, said to have been the great-granddaughter of Nancy's father, who was killed in the battle of Bunker Hill. Her account is the chief source of information of the early part of the story.

The tale of Nancy's tragedy begins in the year 1778, when a tired, bedraggled traveler of slight but erect build entered the tiny village of Dartmouth. His appearance was that of a poor man, but an "indescribable air of good-breeding" set him aside from the usual run of tramps who from time to time visited the area.

Approaching a farm house, he decided to knock at the door and offer his services if a job could be found for him. A middle-aged woman answered his knock, and he bowed deeply.

"I am looking for honest work," he explained.

"Come inside," was the woman's answer. "My husband has just returned from the field and might be able to help you."

The husband stepped into the room, and when he learned that the slenderly built traveler needed work, he explained that the man should apply at the farmhouse of Colonel Joseph Whipple, who lived half a mile away.

"I heard that two of his hands enlisted today, and he might be able to hire you."

The farmer told the visitor, Henry Lorrimer, that he should follow the path outside the house until he came to a deeply-rutted road. There he should turn to the right. Colonel Whipple's residence was the first frame house he would reach, and the colonel was the richest man in the countryside.

Henry thanked the farmer and was given a mug of cool water and a piece of brown bread. After finishing his repast, he started out for Colonel Whipple's residence.

It was nearly sunset when he reached the Whipple farm-house, and Henry was very tired. He had observed the Crystal Hills in the southeast as he hiked, while off to the southwest the blue Franconia Mountains were visible. Slowly rising smoke from a dozen widely scattered chimneys enhanced the countryside vista.

Henry knocked at the door, and a pretty girl dressed in blue homespun answered.

"Colonel Whipple's daughter, I presume?"

"No, I am Nancy, one of the help."

He explained why he was at the door and asked if he could

talk with Colonel Whipple. Nancy went to fetch her employer, who soon appeared.

"Good evening," said the colonel. "How may I help you?"

"I wish work and have walked all the distance from Boston to obtain it," explained Henry.

The two men engaged in conversation, during which Colonel Whipple discovered Henry's name and that, although Henry was willing, he knew nothing of farm life. However, the colonel accepted him on trial and told him to be on hand for the prayer service at eight. Henry was then sent to the kitchen to have supper, which consisted of boiled ham, venison, brown bread, and milk. As he finished, the clock struck eight and the occupants of the house filed into the room. Besides the colonel, there were Mrs. Miller, the housekeeper; two farm hands; and Nancy.

Colonel Whipple opened the Bible and read the Fifty-first Psalm by the illumination of Mrs. Miller's candle. After a simple prayer he gave the benediction, and then the two farm hands left for bed.

Nancy also retired for the night, after which Mrs. Miller showed Henry to his room. Five minutes later he was asleep on a feather bed.

The next morning Henry was given both indoor and outdoor tasks. His body was as frail as a woman's, and his accomplishments soon showed the housekeeper that he was more help in the kitchen than in the yard. Thus Henry often worked alongside Nancy indoors, and they enjoyed "each other's society."

One day a thunderstorm approached just as the farmers were gathering hay. The help of everyone on the farm was needed to get the hay into the barn before the rain began. Henry's hands were soon blistered by his unaccustomed use of the scythe.

The very next day Mrs. Miller faced a minor emergency. The raspberry patch was threatened by a windstorm that would "shake 'em all off," and she sent Nancy and Henry to pick the fruit. They were successful in getting several quarts of berries, but finally Henry's blistered hands bothered him so much that he sat down to rest.

"I wonder why your hands blister while the other men's hands are not affected," mused Nancy, as she sat down beside him.

Henry explained that he was not used to farming and that he originally came from Devonshire, England. Surprised, Nancy told him that she, too, had crossed the ocean from Devonshire to settle with her family in Charlestown. Her father had been killed at Bunker Hill, and their house had been burned. Nancy's mother had died of grief several weeks later. Colonel Whipple, her father's friend, was willing to adopt Nancy, but she was independent and preferred to join his household as a servant.

Henry then confessed that he had a very dark past, involving card playing and fighting. His father was French, of "brilliant exterior but thoroughly selfish," and had married his mother for her money. She died of consumption when Henry was seven, and by the time he was ten his father had squandered all her wealth and left the country.

His mother's brother adopted Henry, sent him to Eton, and for a time all went well. Then his father's "untamed blood" showed in Henry's veins, and he neglected his studies.

When his next quarterly allowance came, he ran away to Dover, signed on an American ship, landed in New York, and there he left the vessel. Henry then wrote to his uncle, who responded with a farewell sum of three hundred pounds and a note stating that "the vile French blood of your father will probably be your ruin."

Henry took up card playing and soon was desperately in danger of financial disgrace. He wagered everything on one throw of the dice, and when he lost attempted to stab his opponent with a stiletto. Henry was forcibly restrained until he calmed down, and the next morning he decided to leave New York. He hiked north until he reached Massachusetts, from where he decided to head for the mountains of New Hampshire. He had ended his lengthy walk at Colonel Joseph Whipple's farmhouse.

By the time his long tale was concluded, both Henry and Nancy realized that they should get back to the housekeeper with their raspberries, for Mrs. Miller would begin to wonder. Before they left the berry patch, however, they decided that they were more than just interested in each other.

The weeks went by and what the farmers called Royal October "stained the vast forests with a thousand shades and tints. Mount Agiochook was already snow-capped."

One day a load of apples arrived at Mrs. Miller's kitchen, and had to be "festooned," that is, cut up and strung to dry for the winter. Of course, Nancy and Henry were chosen for the task, and all day long and into the evening they cut and strung the fruit. Mrs. Miller visited them long after darkness had fallen, and they were still cutting and stringing.

"I'd help you, but two's company and three is not," she said, and left them.

Prompted by Mrs. Miller's comments, Henry and Nancy agreed that they were very fond of each other, and before the night was over they had made plans to marry. The entire farm was informed of their decision, and soon a definite date for the marriage was arranged.

Of course, the countryside reacted to the engagement. One of the most outspoken was old Dame Wentworth, relative by marriage to Governor Benning Wentworth of Portsmouth, who at sixty-three had married twenty-year-old Martha Hilton.

"There's my son John at six feet two," she complained. "She could have had him last year and been Mistress Wentworth. She has thrown herself away on this slim boy. Well, she won't live to see the day when she'll wish she had married my boy instead," she finished with far more truth than she realized.

Nancy's plans now involved a trousseau, and she thought at once of the Indian friend whom she had nursed through typhoid fever. The Indian lived in Lancaster, nine miles away. She was an excellent seamstress and had promised that she would make Nancy's wedding dress when the time came. Nancy decided to go to Portsmouth, purchase the cloth for her gown, and take it to Lancaster for the fitting. She had saved a substantial sum while working for Colonel Whipple, and she took a modest portion of it when she left Dartmouth.

Nancy journeyed to Portsmouth by horseback on October 27, obtained the cloth for her wedding dress, and was back in Dartmouth two days later. She was now ready for the ride to Lancaster. As Henry was needed on the farm, a hired man was to go with her. It was just two weeks before the wedding when they galloped away from the farmhouse. The couple's new home was finished and furnished, and except for her wedding gown, Nancy's sewing was complete. It was now the middle of November and the trees were bare, but the day was warm and bright. A squirrel ran across their path, and every so often a deer would be seen. As they neared Lancaster the distant ring of a woodcutter's axe was heard and then faded away in the distance.

Meanwhile, matters were taking a turn that eventually would spell disaster.

Colonel Whipple had an important business transaction in Portsmouth which he had to attend to in person within ten days. As the weather was so favorable, he decided to leave within a few hours and asked Henry if he would like to accompany him. Henry answered in the negative and returned to his room, where he had put Nancy's relatively small fortune in gold and currency. But his restless mind suddenly became overwrought; he wondered if the colonel had already started out.

Going to the barn, he found his employer about to saddle his horse and finished the task for him.

"Sure you'll not change your mind?" questioned the colonel. Henry hesitated. He thought of the glamour of the relatively large community of Portsmouth and of the money with which Nancy had entrusted him.

The colonel climbed into his saddle. He looked at Henry and asked, "Are you sure you don't want to come along?"

"I'll go!" cried Henry. "Just give me a minute." He rushed up to his room, then flooded with sunlight, and placed all Nancy's wealth into a money belt, which he secured around his waist. Ten minutes later the two men galloped away from the Whipple farm, just as Nancy had done several hours earlier.

Meeting Deacon Hiram Piper on the horsepath, they asked him if they could get him anything in Portsmouth, but the deacon told them there was nothing he needed as he was on his way to Lancaster.

Hours later Henry found himself wondering whether the Devil had made him go to Portsmouth with the money, but by the time the two men entered the outskirts of the town he had convinced himself that he had taken the money to prove that the Devil and his father's bad blood would not win out this time. He would return with the money to his beloved Nancy, confess that he had for a few hours given in to the Devil, and all would be well again.

But it was not to be.

The colonel and Henry stopped for the night and camped. They would continue to Portsmouth early the next morning. Meanwhile Deacon Piper reached Lancaster and saw Nancy on the street as she was leaving the seamstress's home. He asked her how long Henry was staying in Portsmouth.

"That's the first I've heard he was there," Nancy replied, and she began to feel afraid. Bidding good-bye to the deacon, she hurried over to the seamstress, told her to put the finishing touches to the wedding dress, donned her bonnet and cloak, and with a few almost frantic farewells, started out for home. She could not go by horseback, for the farm hand had ridden to Northumberland and was not due back until after dark.

Nancy had often hiked the distance of nine miles to Dartmouth and decided to walk. She started out at once, reaching Colonel Whipple's residence in less than three and a half hours. Of course Mrs. Miller was flabbergasted to see her.

"What message did Henry leave for me?" were Nancy's first words, and Mrs. Miller explained that the colonel needed him and Henry had finally decided to go.

Nancy, strangely suspicious, went to her room and found no note from her lover. Then she opened Henry's door and went to the hiding place where he had secreted her gold and certificates. The hiding place was empty!

Running down to the housekeeper, Nancy explained that she must find Henry. Mrs. Miller warned her that not only had he been gone for ten hours but that the weather was likely to change.

Nancy was firm and said that her entire future might depend on what would happen in the next few hours. Bundling herself up for another hike, for every horse was out of the stables, she explained that she knew where the colonel always stopped as a halfway mark for the night, and she said she could easily reach that campsite before the men started for Portsmouth.

Mrs. Miller tried to prevent Nancy from leaving, but the girl, desperate in her knowledge that the money was missing, believed that the only way she could solve the problem was to reach her lover at the campsite. Taking a few slices of bread, she started off on her perilous errand.

Dartmouth was soon miles behind her. If it had not been for the mission she was on, Nancy would have enjoyed her trip through the forest. An hour went by, the sun set, and it grew colder. Nancy didn't notice that the stars were not out until a stray snowflake chilled her cheek.

For half an hour more she made good progress, but then the storm hit in earnest. Stumbling and slipping as the snow beat down on her, she was soon barely able to walk. Suddenly the snow stopped and the waning moon broke through the clouds.

Nancy's heart gladdened, but then the moon vanished and the snow started again. The storm soon became more violent than before. As the girl trudged along she thought she could hear the cry of wild beasts even above the gale. A huge branch fell across her path, and she climbed over it. The whistle and roaring of the wind through the trees began to frighten her. The cold grew more intense against her snow-covered body, and she longed to rest briefly in the partial shelter of a towering rock; she knew that if she did she would never get up.

Finally Nancy reached the gateway to Crawford Notch itself. The first part of her journey was finished. Praying aloud for renewed strength, she picked up a sturdy tree branch and used it for a staff. Even with this aid she slipped from time to time on the snow-covered rocks. The trees were obscured from view by the driving snow, but she heard the increasing roar of the Saco River and was able to use it for her guide. She kept on, walking close to the river bank. Suddenly she slid down on her hands and knees into the stream. Trembling and crying, Nancy fought her way back up to the bank, crawling painfully over the boulders to safety.

The storm continued and drifts started to pile up. Nancy's teeth began to chatter and her hands became numb. Her wet clothes slowly froze, but she fought on, hoping to reach the campfire at any moment.

Then, in spite of the drifts and the wind, she finally recognized her surroundings as the clearing she was seeking. Surely enough, there ahead was a dark spot from the campfire on the snowy ground, but Henry and Colonel Whipple were no longer there. Nancy scrambled forward and reached the spot, where a few embers still glowed in the ashes. Perhaps she could kindle a warming blaze. The falling snow prevented this, however, and soon all was blackness.

It was then that hope died for Nancy. Nevertheless she plunged ahead into the storm. A mile beyond the campsite she stumbled and sank to her knees. Her head dropped to her breast, and numbness overwhelmed her.

Realizing that she would freeze to death unless she kept moving, the girl tottered to her feet again to continue the hopeless journey in pursuit of her loved one. Her brain grew confused as she staggered through the woods, but she was able to notice that she was approaching a brook. She sank down, grasping a small tree at the brook's edge, and then she leaned her head against the tree. There Nancy succumbed to the fatal drowsiness and died at the edge of the brook that now bears her name.

The snowstorm ended before dawn, and a group of Dartmouth farmers discovered the frozen body of the girl who had followed her faithless lover even at the cost of her life.

The news of Nancy's death eventually reached Henry and Colonel Whipple in Portsmouth. Henry had found a gambling location in that town and had been ready to win untold riches with Nancy's money, but the Devil was not with him and he had lost everything again. This time, however, he did not attack those who gambled with him, and the next morning he sadly started back for Dartmouth with Colonel Whipple, who was unaware of Henry's activities of the night before. Returning home, the two men made arrangements for Nancy's funeral. The Indian seamstress, on hearing of the death of her good friend, journeyed to Dartmouth and was allowed to garb Nancy in the beautiful wedding dress she was never to wear in life. Then Nancy was buried in the village graveyard.

Henry, whose real surname was St. Dennis, soon became dissatisfied with his job and with himself. He took his meager savings and hiked to Boston. He signed on as a sailor on a merchant ship and was lost overboard at sea in a gale several months later.

CHAPTER 6

A CLAMBAKE

In the 1930s, before World War II threatened, for a period of four years I organized and ran real old-fashioned clambakes on various islands in Boston Harbor. Calf Island, named for Robert Calef, a principal in the Cotton Mather witch controversy,* was my favorite location, and during that period we enjoyed at least forty delightful clambakes there.

Early in the morning on the day of the scheduled event a group of us would dig about 2000 clams, clean them thoroughly, and then store them in a cool cellar. A few hours later I would send two trusted youths out to Calf Island in my canoe, with nothing but their own lunches and a few matches.

On the island, the boys would gather enormous piles of driftwood of all sizes down on the beach at the site of the bake, and then start collecting rockweed from the low-tide ledges until they had more than we would need. Next they would scoop a depression in the gravel at least twelve feet across and start lining it with smooth-surfaced beach stones and rocks. Once the stones were firmly set into the depression, tiny branches and hay from the island were loosely packed on top of them, followed by faggots and small sticks. Then driftwood

* See my *Supernatural Mysteries*, pages 48–57.

79

about the size of relatively tiny timbers was added, on top of which coconut-sized stones and rocks were carefully piled. Finally came a special layer of quickly combustible wood.

After all this, the boys applied the matches, and within a period of from half an hour to forty minutes the entire mass would usually have burned and settled down to resemble a miniature volcanic crater, with the stones deep in the midst of the glowing embers.

If all went well, our boat would just have docked at Calf Island Pier, and we would hurry our supplies down over the bank and onto the shore at the site of the bonfire. The clams were brought over in buckets, along with sweet potatoes and corn, and a canvas tarpaulin was made ready.

At this point two rakes were used to pull over and remove the last embers, and the pile of rockweed, which had been kept in the shade, was hurried forward and spread on top of the white-hot rocks. Then the sweet potatoes were spread out over the steaming rockweed, followed by the corn. Next the buckets containing the glistening white clams were placed around the edge of the pit. At a given signal everyone grabbed a bucket and poured the clams right into the waiting steam. These were raked into an even pile; the canvas tarpaulin was raised over and then lowered onto the entire affair; more seaweed was added; and another set of rocks was used to weigh down the sizzling entirety, so that the sweet potatoes, the corn, and the clams all would get full benefit of the steam rising from the scalding-hot rocks below.

That done, a critical decision lay just ahead. The bake was steaming away and the clams eventually would begin to show signs of almost being ready, but what about the corn and potatoes? How long before they would be cooked thoroughly?

There was only one way to find out. (Actually, I have attended clambakes—I'll not reveal where—that were not properly managed. After the tarpaulin was removed and everything was handed out, it was discovered that the potatoes were not ready, the corn only half cooked, and, although the clams were edible, they didn't have that delightful ability to slip down your gullet that properly steamed clams have.) We would always wait a full hour before the first approach to moving the tarpaulin. At that exact end of the hour', every member of our group was alert. About three minutes after the full hour had elapsed, the clambake master would order a corner of the tarpaulin slightly raised and shove his gloved hand into the steaming mass, withdrawing as fast as possible a clam, a potato, and an ear of corn. Only then would he make his decision. Usually all was well, and everyone would be served within a few minutes. However, if the sweet potatoes needed another few minutes, we would wait ten minutes more. But then everything came off and dinner was served!

As the clambake enthusiasts were eating, watermelons were brought down and cut for dessert at the end of the feast.

Of course all has changed since those days. It is practically impossible to conduct a clambake today as in the 1930s, and more than thirty years ago I reverted to Colonel Ezekial Cushing's method of serving clams, called Clam Boil. Now, as in the days of Colonel Cushing, a leading personality of Casco Bay two hundred years ago, everyone drinks clam broth from a cup or large shell. The happy human slips the clam's leatherlike skin cap from its neck and then tips his or her own head at an angle of about $17\frac{1}{4}$ degrees, drops the previously resisting clam down the throat, and experiences pure ecstasy in the process.

It is said that at one Casco Bay picnic held at Long Island in 1883 by the Maine Commercial Travelers' group, the combined length of the tables if placed end to end would have totaled a mile. Of course, apart from the enormous number of clams such a feast would have required, I have figured out that there might not have been enough craft in all Casco Bay to bring the passengers necessary to fill the seats at a table of such length. But it is a good story and I'll not challenge it further.

The greatest number at any of my clambakes was 273, and those of us who did the work were utterly exhausted at the close of that glorious feast.

The author with wreckage discovered during his search for the lost plane of Charles Nungesser

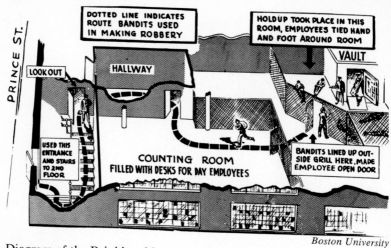

Diagram of the Brink's robbery

General view of the Brink's garage on Prince Street

Left: Joseph J. "Specs" O'Keefe

Large-denomination bills from the Brink's robbery were found in a metal container behind new paneling.

Two views of the Boston molasses disaster, January 1919

Photo by Leslie R. Jones

Looking for bodies at the site of the Pickwick disaster on the morning after, July 5, 1925

A view of the Pickwick disaster on the morning after

Photo by Leslie R. Jones

A view of the Pickwick Club disaster from the elevated structure on
Beach Street, Chinatown, looking toward Washington Street, July 5

Above: The rescue of Lizzie after
the Pemberton Mills collapse

Left: Ruins of the Pemberton Mills
at Lawrence, Massachusetts, 1860

Right: The rescue of a girl by a fire
fighter just before the flames engulfed the ladder at the Pemberton
Mills disaster

Moll Pitcher

Moll Pitcher's cottage

Fanny Campbell, a pirate lady of unusual prowess

The "haunted school-house" on Charles Street in Newburypost as it looked one hundred years ago

Charles Nungesser, a World War I ace who shot down forty-five planes. He vanished at sea in 1927 while attempting to fly across the ocean from France to the United States.

Nungesser's plane, *L'Oiseau Blanc,* on May 8, 1927, a few moments before departure

Right: Smoke from burning oil coming up from the wreck of the tanker *Pinthis* on the sea bottom several days after her collision with the passenger craft *Fairfax,* June 19, 1930

New England's Dark Day, May 19, 1780

An elephant swimming in the water near the burning *Royal Tar*

Two ships of Walker's fleet go to their doom off Egg Island

The *Nancy* ashore on Nantasket Beach

CHAPTER 7

JAMEISON, THE GOOD PIRATE

In addition to a fascinating history colored with tales of piracy, mutiny, and buried treasure, Hingham, Massachusetts, offers much of interest to the historian concerned with the period immediately following the War of 1812.

Every time I visit this delightful South Shore area, I think of the autumn of the year 1951, when Torrey Little and I were exploring in the attic of his great auction barn at Marshfield Hills. We came across a large sea chest he had obtained some months before. On the inside of the cover was a painting of a sailing vessel, the *Molo,* and in one of the drawers a long dirk and an old pair of handcuffs. The sea chest and its contents were all that remained of the possessions of one Nickola, or Nicholas Jameison, whom I call the Good Pirate.

Jameison was a remarkable man, an expert navigator who left his mark on the Massachusetts South Shore for many years. Born in Grennock, Scotland, he was the youngest of thirteen children. His father, a rich clothing merchant, wished him to take up the same trade, but at an early age the boy became interested in the sea. After a liberal education, the youth visited Europe. He was detained in France by the Napoleonic Wars, but his father was able to send him money from time to time.

Following a trip to Waterloo, young Jameison went to sea, and a short time later his father died.

The young man was shipwrecked near New Orleans in 1820 and found himself in dire straits. All that he had been able to save from the disaster were his sea chest, his nautical instruments, and about twenty dollars. Once in New Orleans, he attempted to ship out again.

On July 11, 1820, Captain August Orgamar arrived in New Orleans aboard the so-called privateer *Mexican,* a small schooner mounting several cannon. Captain Orgamar allegedly represented the famous General Prascelascus of Mexico, but several American sailors told Jameison that they wouldn't ship with Orgamar because he was actually a pirate. Nevertheless, the Scot was hungry, worried, and desperate for work. When Orgamar told him the position of navigator was open and assured him that the *Mexican* was strictly a privateer, Jameison accepted the job.

However, once at sea, Captain Orgamar threw off all pretense. After a small Spanish brig was captured, he murdered the crew, took off all the cargo and money, and scuttled the craft. When Jameison protested, the grinning captain informed him that war was war. The young Scot knew then what he was in for and cursed himself for being a fool.

A week later, when another craft was seized, the members of the captured crew were given their choice of joining up or being killed. They all joined, after which the captain set sail for a secluded harbor where a division of booty was made. After the spoils were allotted, fifteen ugly-looking individuals, who evidently had been awaiting the craft, appeared from out of the forest. They signed on as crew members.

Jameison had noticed that the crew was getting hard to manage. Apparently Orgamar, brutal enough himself, was in danger of losing control of his vessel to a band of outlaws who practiced even less restraint. Jameison felt that a showdown between Orgamar and his ruffian crew was imminent, and indeed the Scot did not have long to wait. Two nights later, under a full tropical moon, five crewmen went below, grabbed Captain Orgamar from his bunk, and hauled him up on deck.

"Sorry, Orgamar, but I am taking over as the new captain," said their leader, a cutthroat named Jonnia. "You must decide either to join the crew with me as your commander, or to be set adrift in an open boat."

"I choose the open boat," said the captain, acting as dignified as he could under the humiliating circumstances. His sea chest and a few provisions were then put in a boat, and he was set adrift.

Jameison begged to be allowed to go along with Orgamar, but the pirates all laughed at him.

"We need you as navigator, as you well know," was all that Jonnia would say.

Now began a period of terrorism at sea. Whereas Orgamar had seized only Spanish ships, the mutineers declared vessels of all nations subject to capture and sinking. The savagery of the pirates increased with each new encounter.

Finally Jameison had all he could stomach. During one particularly vicious assault, he objected openly to Captain Jonnia's acts and, for his insubordination, was struck and beaten with a cutlass, receiving terrible wounds about his head and shoulders. He was then tied to the mast along with many victims from the captured craft.

"Which do you choose, obedience or death?" Jonnia asked him. Jameison, knowing his worth to the pirates as navigator, gambled on defiance.

"Captain Jonnia, I want to live, of course, and you need me as navigator. I'll stay on, change my name, grow a beard, and keep quiet in front of others you may capture. But, I warn you now, I'll jump ship if I get the chance."

Impressed by the frankness of Jameison's speech, Captain

Jonnia thought it over for a moment and then decided to go along, at least until he got a new navigator. Jameison now became Nickola Monacre.

The weeks went by and, as vessel after vessel was captured and scuttled, the captain forgot both the episode and his intention to find a new navigator.

On December 21, 1821, the pirates were off Cape Cruz, Cuba, when they sighted an American schooner bearing down on them from northern waters. It was the 107-ton *Exertion*, owned by Joseph Ballister and Henry Farnam, which had left her home port of Boston on November 13, 1821, bound for Trinidad, Cuba, with a heavy cargo of foodstuffs, furniture, and other commodities aboard. Total value of the cargo was eight thousand dollars. The master was Captain Barnabas Lincoln of Hingham, Massachusetts; the mate, Joseph Brackett of Bristol, Maine; the cook, David Warren of Saco, Maine; and there were four seamen: Thomas Goodall of Baltimore, Thomas Young of Orangetown, George Reed of Scotland, and Carl Francis de Suze of Saint John's, Newfoundland.

From the deck of the *Exertion,* Captain Lincoln studied the *Mexican* with his spyglass and realized that he was outgunned and outmanned. He had six men in his crew against forty on the *Mexican*. He decided to surrender without a fight. The two schooners hove to side by side. The pirates ordered Captain Lincoln to report aboard the *Mexican*, but when the *Exertion*'s boat was "hove out" it filled with water and sank at once.

The buccaneers sent over their own boat and Captain Lincoln was taken aboard the *Mexican*. There he shook hands with Captain Jonnia, who told him he had been detained by a Mexican government privateer. Jonnia said there would be a few formalities and then he would be freed. Of course, Jonnia had not the slightest intention of keeping his word. The pirates took over the *Exertion* and the Americans were made prisoners.

Captain Lincoln stood by helplessly and watched as his trim schooner was looted and the members of his crew were shackled in irons. When the pirates attempted to sail the schooner in over a sandbar, they ran her aground. Captain Lincoln was then ordered into a small boat and rowed a long distance to an island where he was left together with the members of his crew and four Spanish prisoners from a previously captured schooner.

The next day Jameison rowed ashore and introduced himself to Captain Lincoln, revealing his true identity. The two men held several long conversations during which Lincoln learned Jameison's strange history. The *Mexican*'s navigator asserted that he would never be captured alive as a pirate, for he carried a bottle of laudanum with him at all times. After making a vain effort to take the poison away from the pirate, Captain Lincoln promised that he would do what he could for Jameison if he himself got away.

The following day Jonnia informed Lincoln that he needed an extra man aboard his craft and that Carl de Suze,* who he claimed was a fellow Spaniard, suited him. But when de Suze heard about Captain Jonnia's plan, he strenuously objected, rushing to Captain Lincoln with tears in his eyes.

"Captain, I'll do nothing but what I am obliged to do, and am very sorry to leave you. You know I am helpless." The Newfoundlander left the group immediately, and Lincoln never saw or heard from him again.

On January 5 more prisoners were landed on the island, bringing the group to twelve in number. The pirates brought supplies to the captives and announced that they were sailing away but would be back in a day or two. Jameison had a brief chance to confer with the American sea captain. As he secretly

* It is believed that de Suze was a collateral ancestor of Carl de Suze, a leading Boston radio personality.

handed him a letter, the pirate advised Lincoln to place no faith at all in Jonnia's promise.

As the outlaws rowed away, Jameison shouted across in English to the American sailors, "Mark my words, I'll come back if I'm alive. Do not forget what I tell you now."

As soon as he could, the captain opened and read the letter which Jameison had left with him.

January 4, 1822

Sir—

We arrived here this morning, and before we came to anchor had five canoes alongside ready to take your cargo . . . You may depend on this account of Jameison . . . The villain who bought your cargo is from the town of Principe, his name is Dominico, as to that it is all I can learn; they have taken your charts aboard the *Mexican* . . . Your clothes are here on board, but do not let me flatter you that you will get them back; it may be so and it may not. Perhaps in your old age, when you recline with ease in a corner of your cottage, you will have the goodness to drop a tear of pleasure to the memory of him whose highest ambition should have been to subscribe himself, though devoted to the gallows, your friend,

NICKOLA MONACRE

Excuse haste.

The supplies left by the pirates consisted of bread, flour, fish, lard, a little coffee and molasses, two kegs of water, and a cooking pot. The days passed rapidly and the food supply diminished daily. Although the marooned men all agreed to ration the supplies, each morning showed that at least one of their number had been guilty of cheating during the night.

The island where they had been marooned was a wretched

ne. Centipedes, scorpions, lizards, flies, gnats, and mosquitoes made life miserable all hours of the day and night. To add to their discomfort and apprehension their water supply grew smaller and smaller.

Three miles away was another low island connected by a long sandbar to the place where they were marooned. As there were mangrove trees on the second island, Mr. Brackett and George Reed attempted to cross over in waist-deep water, but were chased back by a large shark.

On Tuesday, January 22, Captain Lincoln discovered a hatchet. The next day one of the Spaniards armed himself with a sharp pole and successfully crossed over the bar in water three feet deep. Luckily, he was not bothered by sharks. A few days later they all waded across to explore the new island. Wreckage, which included two lashing planks, several old spars and part of the bow, was discovered where it had drifted from the remains of the *Exertion*. That afternoon the survivors caught an iguana that weighed a pound and a half when skinned, a very small meal for so many hungry men.

The following Friday a vessel hove in sight but, although all the marooned men waved frantically, the craft sailed away without noticing them.

The next day the castaways decided to build a boat from the salvaged lumber. Work had hardly started when David Warren began to sicken. On the following Monday Captain Lincoln noticed that the lad's eyes were shining like glass, and the others realized that the boy was very ill. Late that afternoon Warren motioned to the others that he wished to make a statement.

"I have a mother in Saco where I belong," he said. "She is a second-time widow, and tomorrow, if you can spare a scrap of paper and a pencil, I will write something."

But when morning came, David Warren of Saco was dead. The others carried his body to a suitable spot and buried him there. Captain Lincoln read a funeral service, and a Spaniard named Manuel placed a cross at the head of the grave.

Supplies grew desperately short, but the men discovered some herbs, which the Spaniards called Spanish tea. They resembled pennyroyal in look and taste, although not so pungent, and proved a poor excuse for a full meal.

On Thursday, January 31, 1822, the boat was finished and placed in the water. It was a disappointment, leaking badly. After considerable discussion, it was agreed that only six could go in her, with Mr. Brackett in command. At sunset the dangerous voyage began. Captain Lincoln stood on the shore and watched with the others as the six men vanished into the setting sun. Four of them were rowing. Mr. Brackett stood at the helm, and the sixth man was bailing steadily.

On February 5, the marooned sailors on shore discovered a boat drifting by on the southeast side of the island. Captain Lincoln urged sailors Goodall and Reed to go out on an improvised raft constructed of debris from the *Exertion* wreckage and make an attempt to salvage the craft. Five hours later the pair returned with the news that the boat was the same one they had built on the island, and the castaways thought with horror of the fate of their six companions in those shark-infested waters.

By February 6 the spirits of the five men were completely broken. The provisions were nearly gone. Then, around noon, a sail was seen in the distance and an hour later a gun was fired. The craft anchored close to shore and three men began rowing in toward the marooned sailors. Captain Lincoln walked down to meet the visitors and recognized no one. The leader, a clean-shaven individual, jumped out into the shallow water and raced up to Lincoln.

"Do you now believe Nickola is your friend?" the man cried out.

And indeed it was Nickola. Nicholas Jameison was clean-shaven and happy and he had with him in the boat one of Captain Lincoln's former sailors, Thomas Young of Baltimore. But there was no news of Carl de Suze, who had gone aboard another prize. When the greetings were over, Jameison noticed the cross on Warren's grave and asked if all the others were dead. When it was explained how six men had rowed away for help, Jameison agreed with Captain Lincoln that it looked bad indeed for the missing men.

Captain Lincoln was given the choice of sailing to either the port of Trinidad on Cuba or Jamaica. He chose Trinidad, asking Jameison for the loan of a boat if it was too far out of the way. But Jameison insisted that Lincoln and the others journey with him to Cuba. They agreed to go over to the bar where the *Exertion* had been beached to see if they could find signs of Brackett and the other five men. As they sailed along Jameison explained how he had escaped the other pirates. He had been put aboard a captured vessel as a prize master, was allowed to choose his own crew, and had been able to escape the other pirates.

When the castaways and their rescuers reached the schooner, they found a sail and a paddle they recognized as coming from the boat they had launched and knew then that Brackett had reached the *Exertion*. But there was no sign of the six missing men. The schooner had been stripped clean, for there were no masts, spars, rigging, furniture, food or anything else left except the bowsprit and a few barrels of salt provisions. With a deep feeling of sadness Captain Lincoln finally left his old command and returned to Jameison's sloop. The journey for Cuba began.

On Monday, February 11, they were still sailing toward Cuba when a vessel that seemed to be a pirate craft approached and sent a shot whizzing through their mainsail.

"It's the men from the *Mexican* again," cried one of the Spaniards, "and God help us."

But Captain Lincoln didn't share their apprehension, believing that the craft was a Spanish man-of-war. He asked Jameison to stop and accept whatever the future might bring. But the others decided to fight.

After a brief skirmish Jameison surrendered. Two small, armed boats were sent over from the brig, which proved to be the eighteen-gun Spanish man-of-war *Prudentee*. Captain Lincoln and the others were taken aboard and questioned by Captain Caudama.

"Why did you fire on a Spanish man-of-war?" he asked in English.

"We feared that you were pirates and did not wish to be captured by them again," Captain Lincoln explained, at the same time removing his ship's papers from his money belt and giving them to the Spanish commander. When the documents were examined, the Spanish captain smiled broadly.

"Captain Americana, your troubles are over. Never mind what has happened now. Go below and we shall enjoy dinner. Which are your own men?" Lincoln pointed them out, and they were given the freedom of the deck, but when Jameison was discussed it was a different matter. The Spanish captain decided that the Scot and his three sailors should be placed in irons.

As soon as possible, Captain Lincoln interceded for Jameison. The Spanish captain promised to do what he could for Jameison and requested that Lincoln give him a written statement to the effect that he had been politely treated while aboard the brig. Lincoln gladly complied.

At Trinidad, the American skipper was released and given the cabin of a sea captain to live in while awaiting help. Two days later he met Captain Carnes of the schooner *Hannah*, who offered passage home, which was gladly accepted. The *Hannah* arrived in Boston, March 25, 1822, after an uneventful voyage.

Later Captain Lincoln learned that Mr. Brackett and his party had also reached safety, but Carl de Suze was never heard from again. He also learned that the pirates from the *Mexican* were chased by an English government vessel and eleven were hanged after capture. The others escaped into a mangrove swamp, where it is said they perished. Perhaps one of these unfortunates was the luckless de Suze.

A happier ending was in store for Nicholas Jameison. Over two years after his farewell to the Scot, Captain Lincoln received a letter from Jameison saying that he was residing at Montego Bay, Jamaica. Lincoln immediately wrote and asked him to journey to Boston.

Upon receipt of the letter Jameison packed his sea chest and engaged passage with Captain Wilson of Cohasset, arriving in Boston in August 1824. Captain Lincoln was at the wharf to greet him and took him at once to his Hingham home. At the time the captain was "sailing in trade" between Boston and Philadelphia, and he signed on the former pirate as mate.

Later Jameison became established at Hingham, sailing out of the harbor during the summer months in the mackerel fishing industry. When fall came, he set up a fine navigation school, teaching the difficult problems of navigation to the young men of the South Shore. Many sea captains from Hingham, Cohasset, Scituate, Duxbury, Marshfield, Kingston, and Plymouth owed their early training to the former pirate.

One day a pupil of Jameison's was given a mate's berth aboard a ship sailing into European waters, and Jameison allowed him to borrow his sea chest. When the youth returned in the spring of 1829, he found that Jameison had gone out mackerel fishing again. Toward the end of April, Jameison started out again on a trip to sea but was seized with a fatal illness and carried into Provincetown. He died May 1, 1829, and was buried on Cape Cod.

The boy kept the chest. In 1835 he became an officer aboard the new ship *Molo*, built at Medford, Massachusetts. While sailing back from Europe the following year, the *Molo* encountered a blinding snowstorm and was wrecked at the lonely Faeroe Islands, halfway between Norway and Iceland. The sea chest was miraculously saved and brought back to the United States, where it remained in the owner's family until 1931.

Somewhere in a Provincetown graveyard lie the remains of Nicholas Jameison, the Good Pirate, who did everything he could to help an American sea captain out of his distress over a century and a half ago. Mary Lee Lincoln, a resident of Hingham and the grandniece of Captain Barnabas Lincoln, died on November 12, 1954, at the age of 99 years, 9 months, 13 days. She had often heard this story told by her family, and as a child was deeply interested in the pirate account. On many occasions she related this tale to her relatives, one of whom, Howard Leavitt Horton of Abington, Massachusetts, assisted me in several of the details of this chapter.

~~~~~~~~~~~

CHAPTER 8

THE HAUNTED SCHOOLHOUSE

The "haunted schoolhouse" of Newburyport, rebuilt many years ago, still stands on Charles Street in that colonial town. The structure, a private residence now, was originally a primary school for boys whose ages ranged from five to fourteen. The pupils came from the humbler Newburyport families, the sons of fishermen, tradesmen, and mill-workers, and their clothes were tattered and patched.

When first erected, the schoolhouse was an ordinary one-story structure raised upon a three-foot foundation. It had a pitched roof with four windows on each of the two longer sides and an attic above. At the time the ghost appeared, the schoolhouse was in a state of neglect. The faded green blinds and the peeling gray paint of the building gave it an air of shabbiness, and, all in all, there was something about the school and its surroundings that oppressed the beholder and strengthened a willingness to believe the strange story of the schoolboy ghost.

To enter the school, one climbed the six steps in front and opened the battered door before stepping into a small hallway with two large windows at each end. Close and stuffy, the entry gave off an odor eternally connected with schools. Directly opposite the front door was a multi-paned partition window that looked in upon the schoolroom. To the right of the entrance were two sets of stairs, one going up to the attic, the other to the cellar, where the coal was stored. Both stairways had doors that were usually fastened with a latch.

The schoolroom itself was a large one and held seats for sixty pupils, with a teacher's desk at the right of the room. On the walls were several maps, torn and soiled. Otherwise the walls were perfectly bare; there was not even a closet in the room. It was perhaps the last place where one would expect to find a ghost.

Many have repeated the story that in the year 1858 the incumbent teacher beat a thirteen-year-old boy until he was black and blue, then, after school, threw him down into the cellar, where he died during the night. Whether or not there is any truth to this legend is uncertain, but the subsequent story that the boy's ghost had been seen in the schoolhouse caused considerable excitement throughout Massachusetts.

In 1871 it became generally known that strange disturbances were taking place in the Charles Street School. Peculiar phenomena had occurred from time to time within the building, but no one had paid too much attention because the teachers and the school committee were not anxious to start trouble.

But the two teachers who ran the school in 1870 and 1871 were forced to give up their positions after their lives had been made miserable by the constant intrusion of a strange power they could neither see nor feel. It was not a being they could scold or whip, and it did not appear at stated intervals. It could not be hunted down and destroyed; it was something intangible and malevolent.

Miss Lucy A. Perkins was appointed teacher in the fall of 1871. She was twenty-one, strong and willing to do her duty in the classroom. Shortly after her arrival, the knocks and pounding, said to be manifestations of spirits, began. On one occasion, the sound was so loud that Miss Perkins could not carry on her spelling lesson; the banging came so rapidly and powerfully that all voices were drowned out. The noises issued from the attic stairs and the entry. At times they faded until they resembled the tap of fingers, and again they increased in volume until they might have come from the batterings of a mighty sledge hammer.

In an attempt to quiet the fears of her pupils, the teacher suggested that the sounds were probably made by rats and the wind, but eventually she was forced to give up this subterfuge and admit that she really didn't know what was causing the noises.

One afternoon during the month of January 1873, a series of raps came upon the outer door. Miss Perkins went to admit the visitor, but no one was there. In the schoolroom in front of the pupils' desk was a stove with a cover that was raised by a wire handle. That day the handle was seized by invisible fingers and raised several inches, then restored to its place.

The teacher's bell was often moved about the room. One day before school began, the pupils outside in the yard suddenly heard the bell ringing, though there was no one in the building. When the teacher came down the street, the pupils told her what had happened. They were more frightened at the bell incident than at any of the knockings or the cover-raising episode.

The schoolroom proper was ventilated by a shutter in the ceiling that could be opened or closed by pulling a cord hanging down into the room. The alleged demon often opened and closed the vent for mischief. And any door in the building might slam without warning, although no one could be seen nearby.

One day Miss Perkins heard the door leading to the attic

swing open, and as she went out to close it, two more doors swung open. She tried in vain for ten minutes to catch up with the opening doors. The door leading to the cellar had a bolt; Miss Perkins closed that door and bolted it. Instantly the lock slipped back and the door swung open so hard that it crashed into a clothes hook and received a deep dent.

A weird light began to appear during storms when the sky was heavily overcast. Light seemed to creep in and hover over the frightened faces of the awed pupils.

At various times a strange current of air appeared to circulate above the pupils with unusual speed, creating a noise like that of a great flight of birds. A black ball twelve inches in diameter often appeared in the ventilator, dropping just below the opening and then quickly disappearing. This phenomenon was often accompanied by a terrific rushing of wind around the building itself. Gusts of cold air shot into all the crevices, the entire building shook, and the chimney gave off sounds that resembled the playing of a pipe organ. On these occasions the unhappy teacher and her frightened pupils would sing at the top of their voices, trying to drown out the noises by song.

One afternoon a boy named Abraham Lydston, thirteen years old, suddenly noticed a child's hand pressed against the partition window. He shouted out, "Teacher! Teacher! The murdered boy's hand!" Soon everyone could see the hand pressed against the window pane. Miss Perkins rushed into the vestibule, but in the two or three seconds she took to reach the hall, the apparition had vanished.

Late in October 1872, the murdered boy's face appeared at the same pane of glass. The teacher ran out again, but there was nothing in sight.

On November 1, 1872, the ghost appeared during a geography class and stood at right angles to the partition window opposite the teacher's desk. One of the boys, whose desk was near the open door, shouted out, "There's a boy out there!" Miss Perkins hurried out and saw the form of a young boy standing in the vestibule.

"What are you doing out here?" she demanded of the ghost-like figure.

The apparition receded from her toward the attic stairs. It was the image of a young boy with blue eyes and yellow hair. He was wearing a brown coat, black trousers, and a wide band around his neck of the type used by undertakers to prevent the lower jaw of a dead person from dropping open. The most extraordinary thing about the apparition was that Miss Perkins could look right through it and see the sash and wainscotting on the wall. The ghost was perfectly transparent, but easily visible.

Miss Perkins began to tremble and thought that she was going to faint. As she steadied herself against the wall, the door leading to the attic opened of its own accord, and the figure slowly ascended the attic stairs.

Regaining her strength, the teacher followed the apparition up the stairs and finally trapped it in a corner. But when she thrust out her hands to grasp the boy, they met in the middle of his transparent chest, and all she had touched was air. The ghost began to disintegrate and soon disappeared.

On the following Friday the apparition appeared again and went through the same maneuvers, but this time it also introduced certain innovations. It brought two ghostly friends and spent most of the afternoon hammering away on the attic floor. Once there was the cry "Damn it, where's my hammer?" Evidently the ghost found his hammer, for soon he could be heard adjusting the cover of a box and nailing it shut.

A week later the ghost began to laugh softly in a disagreeable manner most disconcerting to teacher and pupils alike. The teacher asked for volunteers to investigate, and a student agreed to accompany her to the attic, which seemed to be the source of the laughter. But when they reached the attic, the disembodied laugh jumped around them here and there, and they retreated to the schoolroom in great confusion.

By this time there was tremendous excitement in Newburyport over these strange occurrences. A special meeting of the school committee was held on February 19, 1873. Two of the committeemen stated that nothing was wrong at all, though the chairman, who also served as postmaster, decided that there was much to explain. But there was little action to be taken. When the newspapers began publishing accounts of the affair, mediums and spiritualists descended on the town to view with their own eyes the schoolroom where the apparition of the murdered boy had appeared.

At another meeting held on February 24th, it was agreed that Miss Perkins should be given a well-deserved vacation. The school was placed in charge of Nathan A. Mounton, and the visitations allegedly stopped. When Miss Perkins married and moved away, the incident was almost completely forgotten.

When I first learned of the schoolhouse ghost, I went to the Newburyport Public Library and talked with Miss Grace Bixby. She told me that her mother had often told her the story, and suggested that I go to see ninety-year-old George Leeds Whitmore, who had been in Newburyport at the time of the sensational events. After two interviews with Mr. Whitmore I had what I needed for my story.

When I first visited Mr. Whitmore's Merrimac Street residence, he admitted that he knew something about the affair that he had never told before. I was impatient to learn what it was, but he answered, "Don't hurry me, son, don't hurry me. It'll all come to me if you just give me time."

I waited quietly.

"Now, I think that I learned the truth about the Charles Street Schoolhouse and Miss Perkins from Tot Currier, who worked in the shop with me years ago. He's dead, and so is everyone else that I knew then, and I guess it won't do anyone any harm to tell the true story at this late day. Why, that happened over three-quarters of a century ago, didn't it?

"The boys who carried out the hoax, for hoax it was, were four in number. They were Tot Currier, whose real name was William, Abe Lydston, Edgar Pearson, and Ed De Lancy—all dead now. They got the idea for the ghost when De Lancy received an object glass which could catch reflections from the sun and throw pictures on any flat surface.

"It took De Lancy several months to master the thing, but when he did he could shine pictures from within the glass forty or fifty feet away. He really became pretty good at it. The figure he used came out clear and distinct, and when it flashed inside a building, well, it would fool anyone not in on the secret.

"When Ed heard about the noises coming from the schoolhouse he decided to have some fun, so he pulled Tot, Abe, and Edgar into the scheme. Tot didn't attend school, but Abe and Edgar did, and they helped matters from inside the classroom while Tot ran around the attic and the entryway.

"Miss Perkins, poor woman, is dead and gone now, but they sure had fun with her, and it was partly her fault, because she was pretty superstitious. The day she went up into the attic, she actually fainted.

"Tot told me all about it one day in the shop, and he explained how he ran out before she came to. Tot never grew very large, but he really was a little devil. Yes, I suppose the boys were mean to have teased the poor soul that way."

After talking another half hour with the old man, I said good-bye to him, and as I pondered what he had told me, I wondered how many of the ghost stories of the world might have similar explanations. Of course, Mr. Whitmore's tale does not account for the other happenings, such as the stove lid, the black ball, the strange wind and other noises mentioned earlier in this chapter. Can you explain them?

CHAPTER 9

TWO UNBELIEVABLE DISCOVERIES AT SEA

Tales of babies and young folk who are either discovered at sea or who survive and wash ashore under spectacular circumstances have always appealed to me. In other books I have told stories of such events. In *Famous New England Lighthouses* I wrote of the rescue of a baby off the shores of Mount Desert Rock. In the same book I told of another baby who was put into a box at sea. The box was tied between two feather mattresses and set adrift. It washed ashore in a great storm and was pulled up by the keeper of Hendricks Head Light. When he cut it open, the bundle revealed the baby, still alive, with a note attached to its clothing. The child grew up, and the note that told its story was preserved through the years.

The following tale is not in any volume now in print. It begins at Provincetown on Cape Cod.

The seaport of Provincetown, Massachusetts, located far out on the end of Cape Cod, has witnessed tens of thousands of arrivals and departures of almost every type of vessel. Equally at home in the spacious Cape End Harbor, as it was once known, were mighty men-of-war of the eighteenth-century British fleet and the present giant warships of our American navy.

In the year 1803, a trim, eighty-ton fishing schooner named *Polly* sailed from Provincetown Harbor. Bound for Bay Chaleur, an inlet between Quebec and New Brunswick, she carried ten sailors. Among the crew was a ten-year-old cabin boy, Ned Rider, the nephew of Peter Rider, the *Polly*'s captain.

The voyage was Ned's first trip, and long before the tall church at Provincetown faded into the distance he began to wish he had stayed at home, where he could put his two feet on a surface that did not roll. As the *Polly* continued her journey up the coast, passing Thatcher's Island and the Isles of Shoals, Ned became more and more seasick. But as the days went by, he slowly recovered and began to lose the feeling of giddiness. By the time the schooner reached Mount Desert Rock, young Ned had fully regained his enthusiasm for the sea.

The fishermen passed Sable Island and before long reached Bay Chaleur. The fishing there proved highly successful, surpassing the most optimistic hopes. Within a few days the last basketful of salt had been wet and the long fishing lines were back on the reels; the *Polly* had a full hold. Captain Peter Rider ordered the hatches battened down and set his course for the journey back to Provincetown Harbor.

Two days later, early on a Sunday morning, the *Polly* lay becalmed off Saint Paul's Island, some ten miles to the northeast of Cape Breton. As the boat drifted with the current, Ned came up on deck and stood by the rail. He watched the gulls wheeling back and forth over the stern and he listened to their almost plaintive cries. Then he heard a new sound in the distance. It resembled for all the world the lusty yell of a young child, but where could a child be calling from out on the broad Atlantic?

Offshore from the main body of Saint Paul's Island was a

large rock, shaped like a pinnacle, and Ned wondered if the voice could be coming from there. Rushing below, he aroused Captain Rider and told the veteran mariner what he had heard. The captain decided to humor his nephew and agreed to come up on deck and listen to the noise the boy had heard. As soon as he reached the rail Captain Rider paused, but he heard only the cry of the seagulls as they twisted and turned above the stern. He was inclined to dismiss the incident from his mind.

"That's what you heard, lad. It was a seagull, make no mistake. Some of those gulls have a different sound from the others and that is what alarmed you."

But just as the captain was preparing to go below, there was another pitiful cry. This time it apparently did come from the distant rock, and even the captain was impressed with the human quality of the sound. He decided to have two of his men row over to the rock and investigate.

Ned jumped in with the two sailors who had been chosen, and soon the men were rowing toward the pinnacle. Still becalmed, the *Polly* scarcely moved on the glasslike surface of the sea as the men neared the rock.

Five minutes later the rowboat reached its destination, and Ned clambered out. There was nothing in sight at first, and so he climbed around to the other side of the boulder. Then he heard the cry again, this time from a distance of just a few feet. In less than a minute he had reached the spot from where the sound came. It was a small niche in the giant ledge, which was rapidly being engulfed by the oncoming tide. There, just about to start crying again, was a frightened little girl. The tide was coming in. She was in water up to the waist, and it was not long before she would have been swept away by the rising sea.

Climbing down from the pinnacle into the niche, Ned took the little girl by the hand. Carefully he pulled and led her up over the sharp points to the top of the rock. Then, holding tightly to each other, they descended the other side. The men in the boat gasped in astonishment when they saw what Ned had found.

The girl and her rescuer got into the boat, and the sailors rowed away from the rock. Nearing the *Polly*, they attracted the attention of the crew. Captain Rider stood by the rail to receive the dripping child, who was now crying steadily from fear, excitement, and relief.

"Well, now," exclaimed the captain, "how did such a little girl as you get off on that rocky ledge so far from shore?"

The child's only answer was another series of sobs. The cook brought some warm chocolate, and the captain's bunk was prepared for the girl so that she could take a nap. Her wet clothes were removed, and one of Ned's heavy shirts given her for a nightdress. Ten minutes later she was asleep.

The men gathered to discuss this remarkable occurrence. How could such a thing happen? Who would maroon a tiny child on a niche in a lonely rock out in the Atlantic where the tide would soon drown her?

"I'd give anything to catch the man who did this thing," said Mate Ben Smith with a vengeance, "for either he or I would go overboard!"

"In any case," said Captain Rider calmly, as if he had already appraised the situation, "it is true that we don't know how the girl got on the rock, or where she came from, but I for one am not going to try too hard to find out. While we're not exactly fixed for a nursery aboard, at least we are far more human than the critters who left that child out on the rock to die."

So it was decided that the *Polly* would keep the little girl aboard for the remainder of the trip. Shortly after midnight a breeeze sprang up, and by dawn the fishing schooner was speeding along at seven knots, bound for Provincetown Harbor with as strange a cargo as ever a Cape Cod fisherman had taken from the sea.

By the time the *Polly* was abeam of Thatcher's Island, the crew had voted to name the child Ruth, in memory of Ruth Adams, whose father, one of the crew, still mourned her death three years before. When they sailed into Provincetown Harbor and rowed ashore, the astonishment on the faces of the women of Cape End Harbor was considerable, to see a tiny girl step out of one of the boats.

Captain Rider, whose wife had died, lived with his mother and his nephew Ned, whose own parents were dead. It had been agreed that Ruth would live with them, and the child proved a welcome addition to the family. As time passed, she came to look upon Ned, who was seven years older, as her brother.

In the summers Ned went fishing, and in the fall, winter, and spring he attended school. Finally his formal education came to an end, and he took command of the *Polly* from his aging uncle, who told friends that he was happy to retire from the sea and "stay home for a spell."

His interest in Ruth grew, and Ned became determined to discover what he could concerning who the girl was and where she came from. After several years of sailing, he was in the vicinity of Saint Paul's Island once more. He went ashore, but he found to his disappointment that no one lived on the island at all, and so his questions remained unanswered. He did, however, discover evidence of several shipwrecks and later learned that the island had been the scene of many terrible disasters in its early history. Nevertheless, from all he could gather, he decided that the child must have been left on the rock during calm weather, as there had been no evidence of a shipwreck nearby at the time she was found.

Back at Provincetown, when Ned returned from the trip

that had taken him ashore at Saint Paul's, he went at once to his home. Ruth met him at the door and threw her arms around him. Then, shyly blushing, she drew back and looked at him with a new awareness as she realized that she no longer thought of him as a brother. Now about sixteen years old (for of course her exact age was never known), she appeared to be a grown woman.

Thus it was that Ruth and Ned recognized their true affection for one another. Ned explained what he had been doing at Saint Paul's Island and ended by telling her of his failure to find out anything about her.

Having known for years that she had been found at sea on a fishing trip, Ruth sensed what Ned was leading up to when he talked about her background. After a long discussion he suddenly proposed that they get married. She accepted him at once. The entire town turned out for the wedding, and Captain Peter Rider built the pair a new house, one of the finest on Cape Cod. They lived happily ever after, unconcerned by the fact that Ruth's mystery was never solved.

Thirty years ago I visited Saint Paul's Island and learned that some years after Ruth had been found, a lighthouse had been erected on the rock. Located across a natural channel of water from the main part of the island, it is now connected by a cable car to Saint Paul's Island.

Several generations of the descendants of Ruth and Ned now populate Cape Cod, and many others have migrated off-Cape. For those grandchildren and great-grandchildren this will always be an intriguing story.

Another account of finding a child at sea involves one of the most unusual events in the history of the Gloucester fishing fleet. It occurred while the schooner *Belvidere* was crossing George's Bank.

Captain Samuel Elwell, whose ancestor had a phenomenal

escape from death in the great storm of 1786, had indulged in a large Saturday evening meal. When he followed it with the usual early Sunday breakfast, he became so sick that he went below and turned in.

Falling asleep almost at once, he dreamed of seeing a small coffin-shaped box tossing back and forth on the waves. In his dream he attempted to steer the schooner so that the box could be drawn up on board. Time and again he thought he was on a course that would allow him to reach the box, and on one attempt he was so close he could see inside the box. It contained the body of a small girl surrounded by seaweed packed in such a manner that the child was held securely in the center of the container. He made a desperate attempt to get the box but failed utterly. The dream ended with the box containing the girl passing under the counter at the stern of the *Belvidere*.

A short time later, Captain Elwell awakened and came out on deck, but he appeared so disturbed that when the members of the crew saw him they asked for an explanation.

"I saw a child's dead body in my dream, and although I attempted to rescue the box the child was in, I failed, after which I awakened suddenly."

The crewmen advised the captain to forget the incident, saying that odd dreams were often the result of eating rich food. The first mate told him that after eating the wrong thing, he often had similar fancies of imagination in his dreams, and vainly attempted to have the captain dismiss the entire dream from his mind.

Less than half an hour later the captain sat down on a fish box to look out over the ocean. An interval of time passed. Then, quite a distance away, he noticed an object that might have been a box. Passing his hands before his eyes to make sure he was not in another dream, he half rose and gave a shout.

"Look! Isn't that a box?"

The crew joined him, and the captain ordered the man at the wheel to set a course for the box. Minutes later the schooner *Belvidere* came up on it, and several boat hooks pulled the wooden object alongside the fishing vessel. The captain looked down and saw that the box was nailed securely shut. Whatever might be inside could only be guessed at until they brought it aboard.

Five minutes later they had pulled it over the gunnel, and hatchets soon pryed the lid off. As fragment after fragment of the lid was pryed away from the box, the men discovered that closely-packed seaweed prevented them from seeing what was inside. They loosened the seaweed and a short time later the body of a little girl was revealed. She was about four years of age and evidently had been dead a week or ten days.

The remains were lifted from the box and temporarily placed on the deck. The men examined the box carefully and discovered that there were holes bored in the sides of the container. The box, made of coarse hard wood and nailed securely, evidently had been built for the purpose of containing the child's body, with the holes bored to make certain the box would go to the sea bottom.

All agreed that, considering the partial decomposition of the child's remains, the body should be replaced in the box and the box weighted down, nailed shut, and sent to the bottom, since the vessel was not to return to port for at least a week. Thus the child was buried at sea for the second time. Captain Elwell never learned the story of the tragedy that was revealed to him in a dream.

CHAPTER 10

~~~~~~~~~

NUNGESSER AND COLI

The story of Nungesser and Coli combines a tale of the ocean, what is under the ocean, and an airplane that flew over the ocean.

Charles Nungesser was a famous World War I French ace who had the remarkable record of shooting down forty-five enemy planes. Early in 1927 he became interested in the $25,-000 prize offered by French-born Raymond B. Ortieg, a New York hotel man, for an airplane flight between France and New York. Nungesser went to his good friend François Coli, an older man who had also become an experienced aviator during the war and had some long distance flights to his credit. They decided they would use a Levasseur biplane already built, and by adding extra gas tanks and making several structural changes fit it for crossing the Atlantic. They painted their plane white and called her *L'Oiseau Blanc*, or *The White Bird*.

Finally the day came when *L'Oiseau Blanc* would have her tryout. The two fliers went down to Villa Coublay, climbed into the cockpit, and took off. The plane reached a top speed of 105 miles an hour and apparently responded well to all the controls, as both men were pleased with the results.

Definite plans for the Atlantic flight were then made. Provisions, including tins of tuna and sardines, biscuits, bananas, and chocolate, were put aboard. Two giant thermos jugs of hot coffee and three quarts of brandy were also stored on board the airplane.

The morning of May 8, 1927, was chosen for the attempt. The mechanics wheeled out the Levasseur biplane from the hangar at Le Bourget Field a few seconds after 4:30 A.M. Even at that early hour a large crowd of enthusiastic Frenchmen was there to say farewell. Handshakes were exchanged and then Nungesser raised his hand for silence.

"You know what this thing means, and we both do. We are taking a risk, I know, but we are taking it willingly and with all our hearts." Nungesser then turned to General Leon Girod, who had given him his first plane in World War I. "General, if we shouldn't make it, then I am relying on you to bear witness to the fact that we took no unnecessary risks and that we prepared our flight as carefully as it could have been prepared."

"Yes, I know, I know," answered the general, "but you are going to make it."

Nungesser shook hands again with a few intimate friends and hugged his brother. Another brother awaited his arrival at New York.

Just then an orderly hurried up with a message, the latest weather forecast. Coli read it. Nungesser spoke to his companion. "What does it say, anything vital?"

"No. A minor disturbance is beginning to form. We'll have to alter course a little farther northward to avoid it. That's all, if you concur at this time. Do you?"

Nungesser nodded and the two of them took their places in the plane. Off to the west a fire was burning, and from time to time flashes of lightning illuminated the horizon.

At 5:18 in the morning, the engine was started. Nungesser let it run for several minutes before he signaled that he was ready. The mechanics scrambled to pull the chocks away from the wheels, and the beautiful *White Bird* began to roll slowly down the runway. *L'Oiseau Blanc* was carrying an unusually heavy load. More than five tons of weight had to be lifted from the ground off a runway barely 2,500 feet long. Nungesser proceeded to the extreme end of the runway, then turned the aircraft to face the wind. He fought to get every ounce of power from the engine before he released the brakes. The crucial moment arrived. The plane started down the runway, gathering speed by the second.

Halfway down the runway she cleared the ground—but fell back to earth. Then for a second time she rose into the air. She bounced back again, her speed still increasing. Now she was 600 feet from the end of the runway, with possible disaster ahead—500 feet, 400, and then 300—still *L'Oiseau Blanc* held to the ground.

With less than twenty yards of the take-off space remaining, the plane rose slowly until she was ten feet in the air. Still in a slow climb, the plane headed straight for the line of trees a quarter mile from the end of the runway, cleared them, was seen by the crowd for a few fleeting seconds, and then vanished into the unknown. Five minutes later there was a vivid flash of lightning and the thunderstorm began in earnest. The watching hundreds ran for shelter.

On the evening of May 9, 1927, the night after *L'Oiseau Blanc* had left Paris, a special edition of the French newspaper *La Presse* was published. It announced the wonderful news that Nungesser and Coli had accomplished their objective and landed successfully in New York. *La Presse* described the details of the epic flight. It told how all the ships in New York Harbor had blown their whistles and sirens. It stated that Nungesser had landed safely on the surface of the water in New York Harbor without the slightest difficulty and under very favorable conditions. The two men, according to the newspaper, had remained spellbound in the cockpit for several minutes, temporarily paralyzed by the fact of victory. Then they had stood up and waved to the little group of tugs and motorboats that gathered. After this they had embraced each other in sheer happiness. A motorboat came alongside. The two fliers were transferred from *L'Oiseau Blanc* to a motorboat, which took the transatlantic fliers ashore in New York. There they were smothered with ticker tape as hundreds of thousands of New Yorkers cheered them in their auto cavalcade along Broadway.

Understandably, every Frenchman who read the news was excited by the reported triumph of his fellow countrymen.

Unfortunately, the entire story was false.

It is true that a plane was sighted bobbing up and down in the waters of New York Harbor. It is also true that two men were seen in the plane. It is true that Robert Nungesser, the flier's brother, was standing on a New York pier with an American flier, studying the lines of the airplane through binoculars. But that is all.

It was soon discovered that the plane in New York Harbor was an American hydroplane. A French newsman in New York, with a Paris deadline to make, had sighted the plane. Realizing what would happen if the plane were the Nungesser-Coli craft, he took the chance of getting a report out ahead of everyone else. He wired to Paris what *would have happened* had the airplane been that of the French fliers—and then the bubble burst!

What did happen to Nungesser and Coli?

After they left Le Bourget Field that May morning they were joined by four French fliers, who escorted them to the English Channel. Then one by one the French fliers left, each giving a final salute as he returned to the mainland of Europe. The last French soil over which the two men flew was at Étretat, where a memorial was later erected to them.

Shortly after ten o'clock a plane believed to be *L'Oiseau*

Blanc was heard between Cherbourg and Southampton, but the thick morning haze prevented an actual sighting. Twenty hours then elapsed with no report of the French fliers.

At ten o'clock the following morning, a plane believed to be the French craft was sighted in the air over Newfoundland. Another report reached New York from St. Pierre, a tiny island south of Newfoundland, that *L'Oiseau Blanc* had flown over at eight o'clock that morning.

Unfortunately, as the hours went by, fog set in—thick, heavy fog that obscured everything. Rockland, Maine, then reported that a plane had been heard in the general vicinity lying down the coast. The lighthouse keeper at Seguin, Maine, is said to have confirmed the news a short time later, stating that he heard the noise of an engine overhead at about the time *L'Oiseau Blanc* might have been passing above that island. Several other reports came from islands in Casco Bay. Then there was nothing but complete, overwhelming silence, a silence that has continued ever since that May day almost half a century ago.

In Paris the cheering crowds were confronted with a bulletin stating that earlier reports of success were wrong. Mobs formed. Angry, disappointed Frenchmen broke into the newspaper office, carried out hundreds of copies of the erroneous papers, and publicly burned them in a nearby park.

Nothing further was heard of the fliers. The hours lengthened into days, the days became weeks, then months, and finally years.

One day in 1947—the exact date is unknown—Robert MacVane, a lobsterman from Cliff Island, Maine, was fishing in comparatively deep water when something caught on his trap line. He pulled to the surface a piece of wreckage from an airplane. He was then fishing at a point directly off the southwesterly tip of Jewel Island, the next island to the south of Cliff Island.

The water in the region is 96 to 146 feet deep, and bring
ing the fragment to the surface had been hard work. Later a
large mass of the plane was hooked and lifted, but in the
attempt to retrieve it, the wreckage broke away and sank
again. At one point MacVane had six feet of the plane above
the surface.

I was given several fragments of this aircraft and took them
to the South Weymouth Naval Air Station in Massachusetts
Commander Lawrence E. Oliver had them examined, and the
conclusion arrived at at the Naval Air Station was that the
plane fragment was from an aircraft of the World War I
period.

From time to time I journeyed with different groups of
scuba divers to the scene of the find off Jewel Island, and in the
following months much additional material was brought to
the surface. (The efforts of divers Hans Krone of Richmond
Virginia, and Howard White of Kensington, Connecticut,
member of the Harvard class of 1959, deserve special men
tion.)

Miss Johanna von Tiling, of Cliff Island, who has a deep
interest in things nautical, was a great help in our efforts to
solve the mystery of the airplane fragments. Late in Novem
ber 1959 Miss von Tiling wrote to me that David H. MacVane
Jr., of Cliff Island, brought up airplane wreckage from the
same general area on November 24, while hauling traps off
Jewel Island. An airplane section, in one piece when raised
to the surface, separated into several fragments at points of
corrosion and sank.

On September 25, 1960, Robert MacVane "again tangled
with the wreckage and pulled to the surface some twisted
fragments of metal described by Miss von Tiling as "grayish
except where chaffed, where it looks greenish." The location
was in eighteen to twenty fathoms of water about 700 yards

southwest of a buoy that had been placed for me the year before.

A visitor to Cliff Island, who wishes to remain anonymous, brought the entire mystery into sharp relief some time later. Tremendous publicity all over America and Europe developed. The visitor, a former member of the French World War II resistance forces, was of the opinion that the fragments, which were on exhibition at Cliff Island, could easily have been from the Nungesser-Coli plane. I went out to Cliff Island and brought a piece of the latest find back to Boston.

Major Marc Palabaud of the French air force and Charles D. Pampelonne, the French consul in Boston, visited the offices of the Quincy, Massachusetts, *Patriot Ledger* to examine the fragment. After several hours of inspection, Major Palabaud asked for and received the fragment, which was sent across the ocean to France for an exhaustive examination.

On February 11, 1961, *Paris Match* published a lengthy article with many pictures about the Nungesser-Coli flight and the subsequent discovery of airplane fragments off Jewel Island, Maine. *"ILS AVAIENT BATTU LINDBERGH"* was the banner headline. The theme that "they had beaten Lindbergh" was stressed, for if the fragments found in United States territorial waters were definitely from the Nungesser plane, then the two Frenchmen had crossed the Atlantic from Paris before Lindbergh's flight, only to crash off the rugged coast of Maine. The *Match* article was buoyant and hopeful that the mystery might soon be cleared up.

A short time later word came from D. Foster Taylor of the J. H. Taylor Foundry Company in Quincy, Massachusetts, that he and his son, David Taylor, had tested fragments from the plane and were of the opinion that it could not be the Nungesser plane. When they fractured a piece of the metal, it did not appear to have crystallized sufficiently for the time that had passed. They stated definitely that the material was not corroded enough to have been under water for thirty-four years. Later they sent a fragment to the Charles Batchelder Company of Botsford, Connecticut, and received a letter from John Dougherty of that company.

Mr. Dougherty stated, on February 6, 1961, that a "spectographic analysis reveals the sample to be 2024 (24 S) Ross Aluminum Alloy of the following composition:

Copper	4.80	Manganese	.71	Tin	.00
Iron	.25	Magnesium	1.58	Chromium	.00
Silicon	.13	Nickel	.00	Lead	.00
Zinc	.01	Titanium	.01		

"This alloy has been used extensively in aircraft for many years," stated Mr. Dougherty. "Its high copper content gives it relatively low corrosion resistance, which fact would seemingly rule out any marine application and tend to bolster the wrecked airplane theory." The material was definitely from an airplane of the general World War II period.

Several days after the airplane fragment arrived in Paris, the French aeronautical engineers came to the same conclusion. The twisted piece of wreckage sent across the ocean was not from *L'Oiseau Blanc*.

They agreed with Mr. Dougherty that the metal was from an airplane, but not of 1927 vintage. Chemical tests made on their fragment showed the metal was Duralumin, an alloy of aluminum and copper commonly used in aircraft construction.

The French metallurgists did, however, make an important discovery. Under a thick layer of corrosion and barnacles, the engineers found a row of red letters about an inch high, and were able to make out A, C, and O, possibly part of the acronym ALCOA. The fragment of plane was definitely not of French construction.

It was suggested by the French government, however, that dragging operations be carried out so that the remainder of the wreckage could be brought to the surface. It was remotely possible that the Nungesser-Coli plane, believed to have been heard by the keeper at Seguin, a relatively short distance from Jewel Island, did crash in the vicinity, and a search of the bottom area might still solve a world mystery. The French suggestion was never carried out, however.

Of course, the news that the fragments were not from the French plane brought great disappointment to aviation enthusiasts all over the world who had hoped that the enigma of Nungesser and Coli would be solved.

If the objects now on the sea bottom off Jewel Island do not have any connection with the Nungesser-Coli mystery, what are they? After investigating the matter, I am of the opinion that it is possible the fragments are from one of the two other planes known to have crashed in the area.

The deck log of the U.S.S. *Tuscaloosa*, a heavy cruiser, for April 5, 1944, reveals that while the cruiser was in Casco Bay waters a few miles from Jewel Island, one of the four biplanes aboard was catapulted into the air. On its return journey to a point alongside the ship, the plane spun in at too low an altitude and crashed into the sea. Aboard were the pilot, Ensign K. W. Baker, USNR, and the enlisted radioman, C. E. Duiguid, USN.

The plane capsized immediately after crashing, and although the crash boat proceeded at once to the scene, the boat's personnel did not have time to recover the occupants of the aircraft, which sank at once.

Bryon M. Tripp, who was serving aboard the heavy cruiser at the time, recalled later that the ship was then very close to

land and relatively near Jewel Island. Tripp said that he remembered the memorial service aboard the *Tuscaloosa* a few
days later, after all efforts to locate the plane on the bottom
had failed.

Residents of Casco Bay for many years had also spoken of
the wreck of a training plane from the Brunswick, Maine,
Naval Air Station. They maintained that the plane roared
in over Cliff Island and then disappeared off Jewel Island with
a crash which could be heard for miles.

My letter to the Brunswick Naval Air Station did not produce any affirmative statement that such a plane had come
from that station, but it seems reasonable there was a basis for
the belief in this story on the part of many people. For example, Phyllis MacVane saw the plane as it flew over Cliff
Island and headed out toward Jewel Island in a snow squall.
She heard a crash a few minutes later off the southwest end of
Jewel Island.

On two occasions we went scuba diving where we thought
we might find the plane. On the second occasion we went
down to 134 feet and did identify a plane that the Brunswick
Air Base eventually decided was a B-12 trainer that had
crashed during World War II.

It was a great disappointment that we had not found *The
White Bird*. Of course, I realize the chances that the French
plane *L'Oiseau Blanc* crashed in Casco Bay after having been
heard passing over Seguin Light are relatively small. But the
plane must have gone down in the sea somewhere, as it was
never heard from again. Jewel Island is in a direct line
west from Seguin Light, and the plane may be in the area
roughly bounded by Jewel Island, Peak's Island, Cape Elizabeth, and Halfway Rock Light, located about two and one
half miles southeast from Jewel Island. According to the lighthouse keeper's calculation, he heard the sound of the engine
fade away to the west, and it was apparent the craft was

headed for the mainland in the general direction of Massachu-setts.

There is no record of this engine being heard again, so the plane may have gone down somewhere in Casco Bay in the general area I have outlined. But years and years of search have not revealed its location, and I am afraid that unless some lucky scuba diver visits it on the ocean bottom, or a lobsterman catches the plane in his lines, *L'Oiseau Blanc* will never be found.

CHAPTER 11

~~~~~~~~~~

SHARKS

I

Shark scares along the New England coast occur almost yearly. When a shark is sighted at the height of a summer season, it brings into sharp relief the long history of these dangerous, unpredictable inhabitants of the ocean.

My first encounter with a shark occurred in Massachusetts Bay while canoeing with my wife across to Nahant from Winthrop more than a third of a century ago. As we approached the Nahant shore, Mrs. Snow and I suddenly sighted a giant shark, which frightened both of us. When we first saw the triangular fin, we mistook it for a lobster buoy. But when the shark rolled over on its back, presenting a white belly as its hideous jaws yawned wide, I recognized what it was. As soon as the shark had passed under the bow of the canoe, I smacked my paddle with great force flat against the surface of the water, which made a sound like a rifle shot. This ruse must have worked, for the shark swam away rapidly, making us very happy. We were even more elated when a shark was captured the next day and brought in to Merryman's Wharf, Winthrop. We viewed the remains and both agreed it could have been the same shark.

On another occasion, when Minot's Light off Cohasset, Massachusetts, was still a manned lighthouse station, I was about to dive from the tower into the sea, but the keeper warned me that there was a sizable shark lurking below, perhaps awaiting scraps from the keepers' dinner, which were occasionally thrown into the water from the quarters eighty-eight feet above.

The thought of being the prey of sharks did not fill me with joyous anticipation, but I took the dive anyway, as those who were to photograph the incident were ready for action. On the other hand, I was anxious to disappoint the shark, and when I hit the water I swam so fast that I probably approached my best record for speed as I raced to the waiting boat.

Another encounter with sharks occurred when Jerry Thomas of Weymouth and I were scuba diving, attempting to find several grindstones lost overboard from a wreck of more than a century ago off Fourth Cliff, Scituate. On this occasion the sharks visited us in pairs, simply overwhelming us and causing us to abandon our diving activities. I remember that we failed to find a single grindstone, although the following year Donald Hourihan discovered one at the same wreck and brought it ashore.*

II

We now go back through the pages of time to the year 1826. The location is a considerable distance from the mainland of New England.

On the night of August 27, 1826, Lieutenant Edward Smith was commander of the schooner *Magpie* with a crew of twenty-four. The schooner's fore-topsail was set, with the yard braced for the starboard tack and the foresail in the brails.**

The mate noticed a small black cloud and decided to warn

* See my *Fantastic Folklore and Fact*, p. 229 and illustration.
** A brail is a rope, fastened to the leech or corner of a sail and leading through a block, by which the sail can be hauled up or in as in furling.

Lieutenant Smith. He looked down the hatchway into th
cabin.

"Mr. Smith," he called, "I think the land breeze will b
coming off rather strong, sir. The clouds now look black."

"Very well," answered his superior officer. "I'll be up o
deck in a moment."

The cloud, swelling to tremendous proportions, moved to
ward the schooner. Suddenly, without further warning, a ter
rific squall hit the *Magpie*. The storm came so fast that the mat
was unable to call the watch, and the schooner began to cap
size! Just at that moment Lieutenant Smith was putting his foo
down on the last step of the ladder. As the *Magpie* heele
over, he was thrown into the water and the schooner san
beneath him.

Two of the sailors, caught below, went to the bottom wit
the vessel. The survivors found themselves in the water, swim
ming around in the darkness without anything to cling to. The
were amazed a short time later to see the schooner's longboa
come to the surface nearby. It must have broken loose fron
its position on the bows, but there it was—swamped, of course

Thinking only of themselves, all the survivors scramble
into the boat, causing it to capsize at once. Then they attempte
to climb onto the keel, but since only a few could huddle there
the others clung to the gunwales.

Lieutenant Smith realized that unless the men turned th
boat over and bailed her out, many of them would drown
Under his direction they righted the craft, and two men sli
over the gunwales and began bailing the water out with thei
hats.

Suddenly there was a disturbance in the water, and the tri
angular fin of a shark was seen gliding along less than fifty fee
away. In the excitement that followed, the boat went ove
again, and the men began to fight for places on the keel. A
the shark drew near, one sailor after another would gai

temporary possession of the keel and then be dislodged by a frantic companion.

Smith urged the men to kick in the water with their feet, for he believed that sharks would not attack under such conditions. Splashing the water with their feet all the time, the men righted the boat.

Four men climbed in. All began bailing steadily until they had cleared the longboat of water down to the thwarts, or seats. Twenty minutes more would have been enough time to allow all hands to get in, but a great noise was heard a short distance away, and the horrified men in the water saw no less than fifteen sharks approaching them. Over went the longboat again.

At first the sharks appeared to be harmless, swimming among their potential victims and only rubbing against the legs of the men. At times they would leap about, apparently playing in the water. Then came the terrifying moment when one man felt sharp teeth bite into his leg. An agonizing scream came from his mouth as he felt his leg completely severed from his body.

No sooner had blood been tasted by the sharks than the dreaded mass attack took place. The air filled with shrieks as one and then another unfortunate sailor lost a leg or an arm. Some of the crew were torn from the boat to which they tried to cling, while others sank to their death from fear alone.

Lieutenant Smith, treading water as he clung to the gunwales, continued giving orders with clearness and coolness, and his men still obeyed. Again the boat was righted, and again two men slid over the gunwales to bail her out. The survivors, as before, clung to the sides and kept the boat upright. Lieutenant Smith himself held on to the stern and cheered and applauded his men.

But the sharks had tasted blood and were not to be driven from their feast. In one brief moment, while Smith was resting from his splashing, a giant shark moved toward him, seized his legs, and bit off both of them just above the knees. With a deep groan and shudder the lieutenant released his hold and started to sink. The crew, who had long respected their gallant commander and knew his worth and courage, grasped their dying leader and lifted him onto the stern of the longboat. Even now, in his agony, Smith spoke only of rescuing the remaining few. As he was giving instructions, one of the men in the water tried to get into the boat, causing it to heel to one side, and Smith rolled off the stern. His last bubbling cry was lost amid the shrieks of his former companions. He sank into the ocean and was seen no more.

Every hope died with him. All but two of the crew gave in to despair, with loud cries of grief and cursing. The boat overturned again. Some who had not been too seriously injured by the monsters of the deep endeavored to climb upon the keel. By now, however, they were exhausted from their struggles and soon gave up the unequal fight, not caring when or how they met death. They either were eaten immediately by the sharks or, courting death, threw themselves from the boat and drowned. One of the last to perish was a sailor named Wilson.

Only two survivors remained, Jack Maclean and gunner Tom Meldrum. The sharks seemed sated for the time being. Jack and Tom, who had been clutching the keel, finally managed to right the boat. Maclean climbed in over the bow and Meldrum over the stern. Still uninjured and in comparative security, they began to bail again. After twenty minutes they had lightened the boat and both sat down to rest, exhausted.

A short time later the sharks returned. The creatures endeavored to upset the boat, swimming along and bumping it time and time again. But after circling the craft for a while, they vanished.

The two men, tired as they were, resumed bailing and continued until the boat was nearly dry, then fell into a sound sleep, their minds relieved by their relative security. Day dawned before they awoke to horrible reality. Heat, hunger, thirst, and fatigue settled on the unfortunate pair. They looked out over the water as far as they could see, but only an endless ocean, a cloudless sky, and a fiercely burning sun greeted them. They had no oar, no mast, no sail, no food or drinking water—nothing but the bare planks of the boat.

The sea was as smooth as glass. The hopelessness of their situation struck them. Hunger, the burning rays of the sun, the sharks, and after a time fear of each other almost overcame them.

Then later that morning Meldrum, scanning the sea, saw a white sail on the horizon.

"By God, there is a brig!" he called out.

The two men jumped into each other's arms and were soon laughing and crying together. Waving and shouting, they watched the brig, forgetting everything—their sunburn, their hunger, and even their thirst.

Suddenly the vessel swung around three points* and started on a tack that would take her on a parallel course to their boat, probably too far away to notice them.

In vain they hailed; in vain they threw their jackets in the air. They were not seen, and the brig continued on her new course. The shipwrecked sailors watched a man going aloft on the vessel. They could see him distinctly, but the man paid them no attention in spite of their frantic waving and shouting.

Time was slipping away. Once they got abaft the beam of the brig, every second would lessen the chance of their being seen. Then it was that Meldrum looked first at the brig, then at his companion.

"By heaven, I'll do it, or we are lost!"

* A point is 7½ degrees of the compass, originally spoken of as ¹⁄₁₂ of a quadrant.

"Do what?"

"I'll tell you, Jack, I'll swim to her; if I get safely to her, you are safe."

"What! Jump overboard and leave me all alone?" replied Maclean. "Look at that shark which has followed us all night. Why it is only waiting for you to get into the water to swallow you. No, no—wait, wait, perhaps another vessel will come!"

Both men watched the fin of the shark move through the water about twenty yards from the boat. Now and then others could be seen. Still, death surely awaited them in the boat, too.

"Well," said Tom finally, "if we wait we must die, and if I get to the brig, we will be saved. If the sharks come, God will protect me! Goodbye. Now if you see those devils in chase of me, splash or make some noise to frighten them, but don't tell me you see them coming. God bless you, Jack. Keep your eye upon me, and keep making signals to the brig."

Meldrum let himself overboard with as much calmness as if he were merely taking a recreational swim. Maclean cheered his companion, looked across at the oncoming brig, and wildly waved his jacket. Then he turned to watch the sharks. Seeing three monsters swim past the boat in the direction of his companion, he splashed his jacket in the water to scare them away, but they lazily pursued their course toward his companion.

Meldrum was swimming strongly. There was no doubt that he would pass within hail of the brig provided the sharks did not get him first. He kicked the water and splashed as he swam. Then came the chilling moment when he saw one of the horrible creatures at his side. Frightened, he swam and kicked so that he made a big splash constantly, but he entertained little hope of success.

With a freshening wind, the brig was running faster through the water, but Meldrum was now close enough for those on the brig to hear him. He hailed and shouted at the top of his ungs. Not a soul was to be seen on deck except the man at the wheel, and he was too intent upon his course to notice the call. The brig passed close to the swimmer, and then every second increased the distance between them. Hope was gone, and the swim had exhausted him. The sharks now waited for the moment to dispose of their victim.

Meldrum knew a return to the boat was impossible. He realized that in his exhausted condition he never could reach her. Then, just as he began to offer up his last prayer to God, he saw a man look over the quarter of the brig. Raising both his hands at once to attract the man's attention, he began to tread water. Then to his joy he saw the flash of a telescope as the man on the quarter-deck first aimed the glass at him and then gave a shout of acknowledgment. A moment later the brig hove to and the crew let a boat down. Five minutes afterward gunner Tom Meldrum was pulled to safety out of the sea. The sharks swam away. Within ten minutes Jack Maclean was rescued, and both survivors were aboard the brig. They had won their awesome fight with death.

III

Few New Englanders have heard what in my opinion is one of the strangest shark stories of all times. With the help of author George H. Toole, I am able to tell the tale. Fully documented and sworn to, the account involves the brig *Nancy*, the schooner *Ferret*, and Lieutenant Michael Fitton, an officer aboard the *Ferret*.

Fitton had heard of walking sticks made from the backbone of a shark and wanted one for himself. On August 13, 1799, he was standing at the rail of the schooner *Ferret* watching several sharks tear at the remains of a dead bullock floating in the water. He decided it was a good chance to get his shark backbone. After failing several times, finally he caught a shark on a hook baited with a choice piece of pork. Soon the monster was on deck with Fitton watching as it was cut open.

To the amazement of everyone, when the sailors opened the stomach of the shark, a substantial bundle of papers tied with a string was revealed! When dried and examined, the bundle was found to contain the papers of the brig *Nancy*, which had been captured in the quasi-war with France and England, and was even then awaiting a final court decision on her disposition.

Fraudulent papers, prepared so that the *Nancy* would be declared ineligible for capture, had already been presented at court. When the new evidence was presented, the court stated officially that these papers were forged, and the papers found in the stomach of the shark were certified as the actual papers of the brig *Nancy*. Thus the shark had nullified the *Nancy* captain's scheme.

The jaws of the shark were preserved through the years, and are still on exhibition although the creature was caught 177 years ago!

IV

When in 1946 I visited Keeper Charles Ellis of Highland Light down on Cape Cod, he told me a weird tale of being in a boat attacked by a maddened shark on November 13, 1920. He recorded the tale and I include his unusual story here.

"I always liked the lightboat *Hedge Fence No. 9*. I had about the narrowest escape ever at that time, too. One day a schooner ran into us and loosened our plates. She was a three-sticker and misstayed at the wrong time to crash us.

"It was a head wind and a head tide, and we were out of luck. After sheering off, she dropped anchor nearby, and our old man, Captain James Frizell, told me to row over with him and investigate. We launched a small fourteen-foot dory, and he had the stroke oar. We started rowing for the schooner, and then it happened.

"I saw a big fin coming for us, and all I could think of was that it was too late for sharks to be in the sound—November 13. I yelled at the captain.

" 'I see it,' he cried. Then the shark came up right in front of us, rolled over, and tried to nudge us so that we'd go over.

" 'Hit him with your oar,' I yelled, and the old man brought his oar down on the shark's head. It must have hurt, for the shark then gave up and swam off. But not for long, for after he got about fifty feet away, he turned and I could see his big fin cutting through the water like a knife as he came after us again.

"Then there was a soft thump and we were actually lifted out of water. But the old man was ready this time, and whanged his oar time after time on the shark. Finally the shark decided to call it a day, and sank out of sight. We were both scared stiff, and rowed as fast as we could to the other vessel. But the fish didn't show up when we rowed back an hour later, and we were very thankful. It isn't any fun swapping punches with a fifteen-foot shark at any time. I'll never forget that November 13th."

CHAPTER 12

DARK DAYS
IN NEW ENGLAND

Boston, the rest of New England, and New York have had many dark days noted in the pages of recorded history, but the most remembered years are 1682, 1716, 1780, and 1881. By dark days I mean those when the sky is almost as dark during the daytime as at night.

The first of these dark days in New England was described by no less a personality than Boston's Cotton Mather (1663–1728). A remarkable clergyman and author, Mather seemed at his best when preaching to pirates soon to be swung off into eternity on the gallows. His manuscript "Angel of Bethesda" covers many subjects.* Mather evidently enjoyed writing about piracy, hurricanes, dark days, and unexplained phenomena, and in the manuscript he mentions the unusual cloud effects of 1682, when atmospheric refraction produced strange appearances.

One evening in 1682 at Lynn, Massachusetts, after the sun had set, a man named Handford went out of doors to ascertain if the new moon had risen. His attention was taken

* See Gordon W. Jones, *Angel of Bethesda*, 1972.

by a black cloud of strange appearance. After looking at it a short time he discovered that it contained the figure of a man completely armed, standing with his legs apart, holding a pike in his hands. Handford called to his wife, who came out and also noticed the huge blackness of the apparition. Neighbors soon joined in observing the spectacle. After a while the figure radically changed, and the black cloud became a large ship, fully rigged, with all sails set. It was identifiable as plainly as if the ship were seen in the harbor. To the settlers of Lynn it seemed the handsomest craft they had ever observed, with its high, majestic bow and black hull.

Finally, though the image still remained in the cloud, one by one, the people went back into their houses. Around midnight, the cloud vanished and the sky was clear. Many reliable people in the town saw the apparition and all agreed that it had happened. What it was and how it can be accounted for is still unknown.

Mather also saw New England's next dark day. On Sunday, October 21, 1716, people were gathered in the various houses of worship when one hour before noon, the greatest dark day known up to that time descended on the northeast. It became so dark, according to historian Sidney Perley, that church members could not recognize others seated just across the aisle of the meeting house. They were unable to locate friends unless these happened to be outlined against a window.

A writer of the period says that "one could not recognize another four seats away, nor read a word in a psalm book." Some ministers sent to neighboring houses for candles, not wanting anything to interrupt the services. Others, believing it would soon pass away, simply sat and waited. Still others were ready to believe that the darkness of the last days was settling like a "pall over nature before its dissolution."

A half hour later it grew light enough for the clergy to finish the services. Gathering at the close of the meetings, the congregations talked about the probable cause of what was almost a supernatural event.

For several days the sky had been more or less overcast. A writer of the period stated that the atmosphere was "full of smoke." It descended near the earth when the wind was from the southwest. On this particular Sunday dark clouds of smoke had passed over, and it was thought that the wind, changing to the eastward, brought the smoke back and darkened the land. That was the explanation accepted at the time by many people. Cotton Mather deemed the occurrence of sufficient importance to send an account of it to the Royal Philosophical Society in England, which soon after published it in its *Transactions*.

Darkness produces a peculiar feeling, probably from the mystery which is involved in it. Unnatural darkness, or what seems to be such, usually produces a weird and gloomy feeling in the average person. It often turns a superstitious mind into channels of fear and alarm. And the inhabitants of colonial New England were subject to such fear and alarm.

Perley tells us that the next dark day, Friday, May 19, 1780, is recorded in New England annals as "The Dark Day." On that occasion the light of the sun was almost completely obscured, and a strange darkness filled the hours that "should have been brightest," bringing fear, anxiety, and awe into the minds of the people.

There are many explanations given, but the most reasonable involves forest fires. From about the first of the month, great tracts of forest along Lake Champlain, extending down to the vicinity of Ticonderoga, were ablaze. Also new settlements were being made in northern New Hampshire and in Canada near the New Hampshire line, and the settlers were burning over the forests preparatory to cultivation.

The early settlers of the northern and northeastern portions of New England cleared their land by fire. In the autumn they would select the ground to be cleared. When winter came, they would cut every tree on the lot halfway through waist high, leaving the forest standing. The men then patiently waited for the strong winds of March to sweep through the woods, blowing down the half-cut trees. If they wished to have them fall sooner, the choppers at one end of the area would cut a tree entirely off, letting it tumble against the next one, and that against the next, and in a minute or two, rows of immense trees would be crashing to the earth. In April one end of the huge pile would be set on fire. It would burn until the boughs and the great logs were almost entirely converted into ashes, which proved an excellent fertilizer.

This procedure was good for clearing the fields, but it often covered New England with soot. On the Piscataqua River on one occasion the soot in certain areas was six inches deep, and the air had been thick and heavy with smoke while the fires existed.

At Melrose, Massachusetts, a high hill only two miles from the center of the village could not be seen from Monday till Thursday of the week in which the dark day occurred. Through this period the sun seemed unusually red, as it often appears when the air is dense with smoke. In Greater Boston, on the afternoon before "the dark day," a breeze sprang up, driving all the smoke to the south. This caused the air the next day to be free from dense clouds of smoke, fog, and haze, making it relatively pure, though the sky was just as dark. At sunset a very dark cloudbank appeared in the south and west, where it remained all night. In southern New Hampshire on the same night, the wind changed from the west to the east, and a dense fog came in off the ocean.

When the dark day itself arrived, the wind was from the east. The sun rose clear and continued to be visible for a short time. Then it became overcast. Changing to the southwest, the wind set in motion the foliage of the trees and brought back the clouds.

"Lightning shot its livid tongues, thunder rolled, and rain fell." The thunder and lightning occurred principally in southern New Hampshire, hardly being noticed in Massachusetts. Considerable rain fell as far north and east as Berwick, Maine, but very little south of New Hampshire.

Toward nine o'clock the clouds began to disperse. As the sun burned through, they grew thinner and thinner, and a peculiar yellow tinge settled over everything. Some described it as of a brassy color, while others spoke of it as having a coppery appearance. Doubtless it resembled the "yellow day" that New England would experience in 1881, but without question that of 1780 was much more intense. The earth, rocks, trees, buildings, and water were "robed in this strange enchanting hue," which seemed to change the aspect of everything. A few minutes after nine a dark dense cloud gradually rose out of the west and spread itself until the heavens were entirely covered, except at the horizon, where a narrow rim of light remained.

A few minutes later the sky was as dark as it usually is at nine o'clock on a summer evening. At that hour in the morning the women of Ipswich, Massachusetts, were busily at work weaving. They were compelled to postpone their work for want of light.

Ten o'clock brought rain to Melrose, Massachusetts. The heavens grew very dark, the light that had been seen at the horizon all morning vanished completely. Standing on their thresholds, women looked out upon the dark landscape with anxious, curious expressions upon their faces. Children held onto their mothers' skirts, "their hearts filled with fear." Husbands and sons returned from the fields where they had been engaged in planting and noticed candles in the windows as they entered their homes.

Carpenters left their tools, blacksmiths their forges. Schools were dismissed and children went home for answers to their confusion, but there were none. Travelers put up at the nearest farmhouse until the weird darkness would pass.

"What is it? What does it mean? What is coming?" queried everyone of himself or of his neighbor. One of two things seemed certain to most minds—either a hurricane such as was never known before was about to strike, or it was the last day when the "elements shall melt with fervent heat, the earth also and the works that are therein shall be burned up."

The darkness reached its height shortly after eleven o'clock, and for hours New England was enveloped in gloom. Candles were a necessity to carry out ordinary business transactions and to light dinner tables. At noon it was as dark as evening. Common print could not be read by the best of eyes, time could not be ascertained from clock or watch faces, and domestic work of the household had to be done by candlelight.

Fires on the hearth shone as brightly as on a moonless evening in the late autumn, and the candlelight threw distinct shadows on the walls. At Haverhill, Massachusetts, a person one hundred yards away could not be seen, and one man in a room with three large windows could not see another in the same room a short distance away.

Animals acted as though night had come. Chickens went to roost, tucked their heads under their wings, and went to sleep as quietly as if it had been sunset. Cattle lowed and gathered at the pasture bars, waiting to be let through so they might return to their barns. Sheep huddled by the fences or in circles in the open fields. Frogs peeped as they usually do at sunset, and birds sang their evening songs. The whippoorwills appeared and gave their calls, woodcocks whistled, and bats came out and flew overhead.

Men and women knew that night had not come and that the darkness was due to some other cause, but they were not sure whether that cause was natural or supernatural. In Boston one of the Reverend Dr. Byles' congregation sent her servant to ask what was going on.

"Give my respectful compliments to your mistress," replied the doctor, "and tell her I am as much in the dark as she is."

Ignorant and learned alike feared that it might be a token of the dreadful day of universal destruction. Many were of the opinion that the "sun of mercy had set, and the night of despair, of judgment, and the end of all things was at hand," according to historian Perley. It was popularly believed that the Revolutionary War, which had been in progress for five years, might be to blame. It could be the fulfillment of the prophecy that announces "wars and rumors of war" as coming before "the great and dreadful day of the Lord."

The dark day influenced the minds of all classes. The more excitable persons ran about the streets exclaiming, "The day of judgment is at hand!" almost convincing many that it was true. In several cases those who believed they had wronged their neighbors visited them and confessed, asking their forgiveness. Others dropped on their knees in the fields and prayed, perhaps for the first and last time in their lives. Some sought to hide themselves, thinking thus to escape the "great day of God's wrath."

A party of sailors landed in Salem. Noticing the gloom around them, they went noisily through the streets with bravado.

The legislature in Connecticut was in session that day. The deepening gloom surrounded the capital city, and the State House grew dark. The journal of the House of Representatives reads, "None could see to read or write in the house, or even at a window, or distinguish persons at a small distance, or perceive any distinction of dress, etc., in the circle of attendants. Therefore, at eleven o'clock adjourned the house till two o'clock afternoon." The council was also in session, and several of its members exclaimed, "It is the Lord's great day!" There was a motion to adjourn, but Stamford member Colonel Abraham Davenport quickly arose and with great moral courage and reason said, "I am against the adjournment. Either the day of judgment is at hand or it is not. If it is not there is no cause for adjournment. If it is, I wish to be found in the line of my duty. I wish candles to be brought.*

At Salem, Dr. Nathaniel Whitaker's congregation came together at their church, and he preached a sermon in which he maintained that the darkness was divinely sent to rebuke the people for their sins. In many other towns church bells were rung to call people together for religious services and crowds attended. Parishioners sought their pastors for some explanation and were almost invariably answered by reference to Bible passages such as the following from Isaiah xiii:10:

> For the stars of heaven and the constellations thereof shall not give their light; the sun shall be darkened in his going forth, and the moon shall not cause her light to shine.

The sermons also were founded upon such texts. In the middle of the day, with their families around them, devout fathers reverently read aloud from the Bible and then knelt and prayed. Pious men were sought out by their neighbors for advice.

At about two o'clock in the afternoon, when a moderate rain fell at Norton, Massachusetts, the horizon began to grow lighter. The day still remained as dark as a moonlit night for some time, and housekeepers could not see to perform their ordinary work without the aid of candles until later in the afternoon. As the sky grew lighter, the yellow brassy appear-

* John Greenleaf Whittier relates the incident in his *Tent on the Beach*.

ance of the morning returned, and remained until an hour or two before sundown, when the sun was finally seen again, shining through the murky air with a very red hue.

After sundown the clouds again came overhead, and it grew dark very fast, "the evening being as remarkable as the day." The moon had become full the preceding day and rose at nine o'clock; but in spite of that the night was the darkest that the people of New England had ever seen. It was as nearly totally dark as could be imagined. A person could not see his hand when he held it up, nor a sheet of white paper held within a few inches of his eyes, and the sky could not be distinguished from the earth. Those who were away from home, though well acquainted with the roads, could only with extreme difficulty and great danger reach their own houses, and several persons lost their way in familiar places. Some, totally bewildered, shouted for aid only a few rods from their own doors.

Many of those upon the roads, being unable to see in the darkness, refused to continue. The rising of the moon did not lessen the darkness, which continued complete. About eleven o'clock a slight breeze sprang up from the north-northwest, and a faint glimmer of light appeared. At midnight it was considerably lighter.

When morning came, light erased the gloom and "fear passed away." The people gratefully welcomed the light of another morning, though the sky was obscured by clouds and unusually dark, the temperature low, and a northeast wind blowing.

The darkness had extended over the middle and southern portions of New England, but it varied in density in different localities, being thickest in Essex County, Massachusetts. It was noticed as far west as Albany, New York, north as far as Portsmouth, New Hampshire, and out on the ocean for a score of miles.

What caused the extraordinary darkness of the dark day in

780? Some people still hold the opinion that it was supernatural, but the great majority conclude that it was the effect
of several natural causes coming at one time. I believe that
the smoke that had spread over the area remained for several
weeks and joined a dense layer of cloud and another thick
layer of vapor that had been driven by a lower air current
blowing in an opposite direction under the stratum of smoke.
Beneath this vapor more smoke had arisen in such quantities
that another stratum was formed, held stationary by a heavy
fog coming in from the sea. All of this made a thick covering
blocking out the light of the sun. Where the darkness was
deepest, more soot and cinders were precipitated than in other
sections.

Over a century later, on Tuesday, September 6, 1881, another darkness covered New England almost from sunrise to
sunset. It was similar to the famous "dark day" of 1780, but
on account of the intense brassy coloration in the atmosphere,
reflected everywhere, it has gone down in history as "the
yellow day."

Today, with pollution from many sources, we are familiar
with smog. In 1881, smoke from forest fires was often blamed.
On that particular Thursday the smell of smoke had filled the
air for several days, indicating its presence in large quantities.
Writers in 1881 generally had little doubt that all the dark
days were caused by smoke.

Various opinions were given on the source of the smoke.
Perley believed that it came from forest fires which, it was
said, were then raging in Canada and the West. Others thought
it might be due to an active volcano in the interior of Labrador. Still others supposed it came from the immense peat bogs
of the Labrador barrens, which in dry seasons burn to the
rocks, the fire actually running over them faster than on a
prairie. In two or three days' time such fires sometimes swept
from Hudson Bay to the Gulf of St. Lawrence.

On the "yellow day" of 1881 there was one difference from that of 1780. In the morning there was no apparent gathering of clouds such as occurred in 1780. Early in the morning the sun and sky appeared red, and toward noon every part of the sky assumed a yellow cast, which tinged the entire landscape—buildings, ground, foliage, and verdure—with its peculiar copper shade. All things were beautiful, strange, and weird. It seemed as if nature were passing into an "enchanted state." It was at first intensely interesting, but as the hours dragged on, the sight became oppressive and almost monotonous. Nevertheless, those who witnessed the "yellow day" did not forget it for the rest of their lives.

The day was warm and the air close and still. In certain areas the air was unusually charged with moisture. It was not until almost the end of the day that the red sky and sun reappeared and the darkness lifted.

During the day, lamps were lighted in shops and offices to enable people to work or read or write. Work was suspended in many places, and in scores of schools a recess was taken during the darkest part of the day. In several instances the scholars were dismissed.

In some New England areas people were considerably excited, thinking that a hurricane, tornado, or some type of heavenly activity would follow. It was even conjectured that the earth was passing through the tail of a comet. There were also those who believed that it might be the last great day of darkness before eternity, that the end of the world was approaching when they would meet their Lord. Few of them believed it strongly enough to make any preparation for the event, however. There were also those who suggested that it was a token of divine sympathy for President James A. Garfield, who was then dying at Elberon, New Jersey, after having been fatally wounded by Charles J. Guiteau on July 2, 1881. Garfield passed away on September 19, 1881.

The darkness prevailed over a large part of New England, being noticed as far north as White River Junction in Vermont, some distance into Maine, westward to Albany, New York, and south into Connecticut, where it cleared early in the afternoon.

In October 1917 Mary Fifield King of Boston stated that she remembered the "yellow day" perfectly. Writing about the subject more than a third of a century later, she stated that there was "such a strong color and a brilliant stillness! The big bed of red geraniums in the yard looked almost white. The horse as my father drove into the yard shied at the strangeness."

PART THREE

At Sea

CHAPTER 1

≈≈≈≈≈≈

THE *FAIRFAX–PINTHIS* DISASTER

The disaster that befell the *Fairfax* and the *Pinthis*, even after forty-six years, is still so involved in controversy that just what happened during and after the collision can probably never be determined.

At five o'clock in the evening of June 10, 1930, the 5649-ton steamship *Fairfax* of the Merchants and Miners passenger line sailed from Boston Harbor on her regular run down the coast to the south. A heavy fog soon settled over Massachusetts Bay, and Captain A. H. Brooks ordered the steamer to proceed at a speed of from ten to twelve knots.

The first warning of trouble came at 6:58 that night when the Shell Oil tanker *Pinthis*, of 1,111 tons, suddenly hove in view from out of the fog half a point off the starboard bow of the *Fairfax*.

Captain Brooks, hearing one blast of the whistle, ordered the helm hard-a-port and backed away at full speed. The *Fairfax* quivered from stem to stern as the engine fought to reverse the steamer's direction, but it was too late to avoid a collision.

Coming together with a sickening crash, the two ships b came entangled in each other's girders and plates. The *Pinth* with eleven thousand barrels of oil on board, caught fire a most at once. Blazing oil spouted high into the air, sprinkli flaming fuel down on the two steamers. The *Fairfax* al caught fire and most of her decks were soon a mass of roari flames.

The *Pinthis* started to sink at once. As she began her fir plunge into the foggy sea off Scituate's Fourth Cliff, t blazing tanker slowly pulled away from the *Fairfax*. All nin teen aboard the *Pinthis* perished.

Captain Brooks now cleverly maneuvered the *Fairfax* order to get the fire on her decks into the lee, thus preventi it from spreading. The crew fought their way to the burni section with the ship's fire apparatus, and after superhuman e forts, extinguished the blaze. Several marines and sailors wh were aboard as passengers helped the ship's company beat o the flames and then assisted in maintaining general order.

Immediately after the collision, the captain ordered an SC sent out. Then he anchored the *Fairfax* in a position off t shores of the Third and Fourth Cliff in Scituate a conside able distance from the mouth of the North River. The 5,649-to steamer had sustained substantial damage. Her bows we seriously damaged above the waterline, but it did not preve the *Fairfax* from reaching port later under her own power. A though the *Pinthis* had gone to the bottom, blazing oil fro the tanker lighted the sea for miles around. The Coast Gua cutter *Tampa* was a short distance away, but Captain Broo did not request her aid, because with the sea on fire the cutt would be unable to approach. Also in the area was the *Glo cester*, the sister ship of the *Fairfax*. Alerted by the *Fairf* radio operator, she had proceeded to the disaster scene.

Quartermaster John V. Eubank, nineteen years old at t time of the tragedy, told me years later of the horror th

llowed the sinking of the *Pinthis*. He believed that if a boat
ad been launched after the collision, many more people could
ave been saved. At the Coast Guard inquiry in Boston it was
ated that there were men qualified to go out to the scene
f the disaster from both North Scituate and Brant Rock
ations. When I interviewed him, Eubank was particularly
itter against the Scituate and Marshfield Coast Guardsmen
t each station, who claimed that they had no right to go out
rough the fog to the scene of the wreck and leave the station
northanded without a direct order from a district officer in
harge of the area. Boatswain's Mate James McIntyre testified
ater at the hearing that their North Scituate motorboat could
e used only against rumrunners. Eubank believed this asser-
on was ridiculous, and in this opinion he is seconded by no
ess than six captains of the Boston Marine Society, of which
, holding Certificate #2738, am a member.

Eubank's remarks at the Boston hearing were the most dra-
natic of the day. When questioned by Mr. Lyons, chief federal
teamboat inspector, about what happened after the collision,
ubank answered in his soft Virginia accent.

"I just came off watch. I was relieved two minutes of 7 and
vent to my room. Went down on deck and went up to the main
leck door where you go down to the main deck. I looked again
nd I saw the smokestack of the other ship.

"There was a marine on deck and I told him 'We are going
o have an accident, look at that ship.' By that time she struck.

"I went up to my room. Tried to get to my room to call some
of the quartermasters that were asleep. Didn't get any further
han the boat deck. Almost got to the dance hall when smoke
nd flames came along.

"I started to my lifeboat, which was No. 9, the last one on
he starboard side and tried to get the gripes off of her. As
oon as I got to her the flames were going over her and I went
lown to the promenade deck. The mate came and I asked him

did he call the quartermaster. He never answered me. Th
other quartermaster came and I asked him had he called th
other quartermaster and he said, 'Yes, he is up on deck, he
all right.'

"We both walked down the steps together and walked ove
to the rail. I started forward to go to my stateroom and get
life-preserver. The smoke and flame was heading me off agai
I went back and it got so dense I couldn't see anybody. I be
gan to strangle in the smoke. I started to go over the rail bu
somebody held me back. A woman threw her arms around m
and tried to get me to jump overboard and carry her with m
I loosened her hold. Broke loose from two of them and go
over to the rail and got down to the hurricane deck.

"I tried to go forward again. Just as I started forward m
clothes caught fire. Then I went to the rail and tried to sta
there, but couldn't, so finally I jumped overboard. I used th
log line on the starboard side. I got on it. Five or six were o
it then. I knew it was going to break with so many on it, s
I let go and tried to get on the rudder.

"I missed the rudder the first time. Something struck my fee
It was the propeller. I was sort of dazed. When I came to
saw a blaze about my head and I saw the rudder. Climbed u
on it. I was all right then and I hollered to somebody to com
and get hold of my feet and hang on. Nobody came. One bo
started up but he went down before he got to me. I stayed o
the rudder until the ship started ahead.

"Engines started ahead and went through all this fire and i
got so bad it burned me and I had to let go. The fire was burn
ing so bad I had to dive. I dove and swam under water fo
five feet and came up. I came up in a place two feet square t
get some air. Closed in with fog and I went down and swam
under water for five more feet and I came up again and it wa
all clear. I didn't have any life preserver of my own to use.
saw those people about 50 feet away from me. I made fo

hem. I got to them and it was this navy officer with his wife.
 asked him before I got to him would he give me a life pre-
erver and he said 'yes.' When I got where the lieutenant was
 gave up and went down. He pulled me up and got me in this
ife preserver.

"Floating in the water. I next came to a man who struggled
vith me. I told him to get away from me. I knew if I had
tayed there I would drown, so I left him and got away five feet
or so. I noticed there was somebody else, and saw the waiter
vith his white coat on. I laid his face up and looked to see
vho it was and it was one of the boys named Seeley. I shook
iim to see if he was alive, but he didn't move, so I took his
ife preserver off. It took me twenty minutes.

"I saw this lifeboat afire. I told the sailor and his wife and
hese other two, 'All hands go to the lifeboat.' The only chance
ve had. He said, 'No, sir, we are going to stay here; we won't
go to the lifeboat.' I said, 'Well, I am going.' I made for the
ifeboat. Took an hour and one-half to get there. After I got
here two waiters, two boys, were hanging on. I told them
both to hang on. One of them let go before I could help him.
I managed to get in. Boat was in a light blaze. Took my hand
and threw water all around. Then she was almost sunk and I
started to bail her out. The boy was screaming to me to help
him from drowning. I told him to wait until I got some water
out. If I tried to get him in then we would sink. I got about
half the water out and got him in and told him to bail. He
couldn't bail any.

"We bailed until I got sick and lay down in the bottom. I
fell unconscious. I don't know what time it was when I came to,
but I heard the *Fairfax* blowing four long whistles. Then we
discovered that the lifeboat had started leaking again, for a
rubber bailer had burned out.

"I tore our shirts off and put them in the hole. She had a
wooden stem and was burned through. The water was coming

in. I didn't bother with that. That would make it all the worse. So I took the tanks, some of them, and threw them overboard, some of them half full with water, and I put them back on the stern and got back in myself and kept her bow out of water. Then we started to yell for help.

"One ship passed us and didn't hear us. Then we drifted until about 12 o'clock, when I took a hatchet, ripped a can open and made a sail, a sort of sail which I put up in the bow. ripped some boards at the bottom that were burned and tried to make some paddles. They broke when I started to use them.

"While I was thinking what to do then, I looked up and saw this Gloucester fishing smack named *Dacia*. I started to shout. Joe started hollering. He was too hoarse. I couldn't yell either. So we took a hatchet and threw it on the can and tried to attract attention. Then they lowered a dory from the fisherman and took us out of the lifeboat and brought us in to Boston."

Captain John Stewart of the government investigating board then asked Eubank if a boat passing within a mile radius from the *Fairfax* would have found them, and the boy answered in the affirmative.

Harry E. Kipp was another who testified at the hearing. A marine sergeant who helped man a fire hose, Kipp stated that as he worked with the hose he noticed passengers and crew members jumping overboard.

"I saw at one time a lifeboat containing eight or nine men," he explained. "Five could easily have handled the boat, and do not think they were members of the crew of the lifeboat, for they were sitting in the seats. It had been partly lowered. None of the ship's officers was near the boat.

"Other men were running about the deck creating greater panic among the passengers, yelling and shouting. They lost their heads. None of them had been hurt and they would have been saved had they remained aboard the ship.

"I saw no trouble between officers of the ship or between

ficers and crew. Most members of the crew did very well, but the passengers rendered great assistance in fighting the fire and their extra help may have saved the ship.

"Considering that there were 23 fire lines on the boat and a crew of 80, I don't think the lines could have been fully manned, with nine men in a lifeboat and others below decks in the engine room.

"There was a panic among the passengers from the smoke and fire. Women could hardly be expected to retain their nerve under such conditions. But the nurses were very efficient and the ship's nurse worked very hard. I saw one lifeboat full of passengers but that was ninety minutes after the collision."

A *Fairfax* passenger, Lieutenant J. A. Nash of the U.S. Navy, commented that the officers and crew "handled themselves as efficiently as possible under the circumstances." Nash's wife was badly burned in the flames that enveloped the starboard side of the liner but later recovered.

Passenger Robert French told how at the time of the collision he heard the *Fairfax* sound a long blast but did not hear another whistle. There was no confusion in the engine room when it filled with smoke, according to members of the "black gang" who talked with him later. French explained how he fought the fire on the port side of the *Fairfax*, assisted by an oiler and a wiper.

Able Seaman M. Silvia, a Portuguese sailor from Baltimore, recalled going on deck to get the fire hose and seeing the seamen and mates there. He declared that a woman helped with the hose. The woman, he said, was a passenger.

Able Seaman Frank Grace said briefly that he was not frightened, saw no one who was, saw none leap from the decks, and saw no sailors or marines about. Grace was in his bunk when the crash came. Although the fire bell was but eight feet from his head, he failed to hear it ring. After going to his station at lifeboat No. 3 and finding no one else there, Grace joined the other crew members fighting the flames, until the blaze was extinguished thirty minutes later.

Miss Nellie Toddel, senior hostess on the *Fairfax*, said she saw no evidence of panic but had observed officers and members of the crew assisting passengers to the lifeboats in an orderly manner. Her story was corroborated by Miss Alice Mannix, a passenger; and two maids, Martha Hennaman and Mabel Hermanson.

The assistant chief of the Boston fire department expressed the opinion that there must have been efficient discipline to have accomplished the saving of the steamship.

The officers of the *Fairfax* testified that no ship could have aided them immediately after the collision because the sea was on fire, and ships could not have approached near enough to perform rescues.

The inspectors stressed the importance of establishing the facts regarding the sending out of the SOS call. Entries that should have been made in the ship's radio log were not in the log. There was no entry of any SOS having been sent out within a minute or two of three minutes past seven, the time of the crash. Captain Brooks testified that he gave verbal orders for such a message, and the inspectors called the chief radio operator, J. Wesley Geweken of Baltimore.

The youthful radioman said he was licensed and had been in service on the *Fairfax* for several months. He was questioned concerning the sending of the SOS and stated that Captain Brooks gave him a verbal order that he attempted to carry out but he discovered that the aerial had been burned off. By the time it was repaired, about twenty-five minutes later, he believed the danger was over. He admitted that the captain had not ordered him to cancel the SOS, but he didn't call the navy yard because he knew the *Gloucester* was right behind the *Fairfax*. He reported to Chatham at the time and later talked with the *Tampa*.

Geweken admitted that it was his own decision not to send out the SOS after reestablishing communication, but insisted that he had flashed out the call eight or possibly ten times before he discovered that his antenna was out of commission, and that he couldn't tell whether it had gone out or not.

He said he didn't keep a record of all messages and that he didn't make a notation at the time he talked with the *Tampa*, but did later. His own log showed that the *Tampa* called and asked if everything was O.K., that he radioed back that everything was O.K., and that the *Gloucester* was to take off the passengers. He said the message was signed merely "Coast Guard," and that no name came with it.

"What did you mean by 'O.K.' when the ship was afire and lives had been lost?" shouted Inspector Lyons at the hearing. "Conditions were far from O.K., weren't they?"

The witness answered, "I meant there was no further danger to the ship."

Captain Brooks was then summoned to the stand and questioned as to his qualifications as a mariner. He offered his credentials and stated that he was licensed and was in command of the *Fairfax* on Tuesday, June 10. The captain was asked to tell in his own words what happened aboard the *Fairfax* the night of the disaster.

"At 6:58 a vessel loomed a half-point off the starboard bow," stated Captain Brooks, "and at the same time there was one blast of a whistle. I ordered the wheel hard a-port and reversed the ship full speed. Some 30 seconds later we collided. Almost immediately the *Pinthis* burst into flames. I tried to back out, and couldn't until she sank.

"I was backing all the time, then went ahead to get the wind on the starboard. All men were ordered to their positions."

Later in his testimony Captain Brooks said that some members of the crew had jumped overboard.

"What caused members of the crew to jump overboard? Fright?"

The question was direct. So was the answer.

"Yes."

Captain Brooks was asked by Captain Lyons, "Who was in the pilot house with you at that time?"

"Captain Robertson, the pilot for the Cape Cod canal; A. J Powell, chief officer; J. W. Brooks, the quartermaster; and myself."

At no time during the collision, declared Captain Brooks was there any conversation in the pilot house.

The captain of the *Fairfax* then stated that there were seventy-six passengers on board and eighty in the crew. He transferred fifty-six to the *Gloucester*. Twelve passengers died in the sea, and eleven crewmen leaped to their death.

Captain Brooks' testimony shows that he traveled the 21 miles from Finn's Ledge near Graves Light to the point of collision at 11.2 knots an hour, not a moderate speed in the fair tide then being experienced. Low water was at 5:00 P.M.

The questioning of Brooks continued.

"Now, you had a full complement of crew?"

"Yes."

"How many men did you have on lookout?"

"I had one man in the bow."

"How often are fog signals required?"

"One per minute, sir."

"How long would it take you to stop the *Fairfax*?"

The captain said he could stop the *Fairfax* in 300 feet at the speed he was then going.

Upon further questioning, Captain Brooks stated that when he heard the fog signal from the *Pinthis*, and he heard it only once, he reversed immediately.

"How much time would you say there was between the signal and the time of the collision?"

"Thirty seconds."

"The time of the whistle was at 7:08?"

"That is the engineer's time."

"How do you fix the time you heard the fog signal at 7:03?"

"I got it from the engineer's log."

"Now, were there some statements in the newspapers as to conditions of panic?"

"I never saw any cooler people than were aboard that ship."

"You were in the pilot house?"

"Yes."

"The officers were on the ship where their duties called them?"

"Yes."

"Fire signals were given?"

"Yes, all bells were sounded."

"All members of the crew went to their stations?"

"Yes."

"Did every man aboard know his station?"

"Yes."

"Were the stations posted about the ship?"

"Yes."

"Were you given any assistance by the passengers?"

"Yes, I saw some marines there getting out the fire hose."

"Now, you went about the passengers to see if you could assist them?"

"Yes. Everybody was made comfortable."

"Now, did you hear any criticism among the passengers of the crew?"

"No."

"Did you hear any praise?"

"We heard plenty."

"Do you feel that everything was done by the crew and officers in this emergency?"

"Yes."

"For what reason did they jump overboard?"

"I presume they came on deck and saw it covered with flames and that was the only thing they could do."

"Looking at it now, as the accident happened, can you think of anything you could have done to avoid collision?"

"Not a thing in the world."

"Do you think that if any vessel responded, it could have done anything?"

"No. The *Fairfax* was covered with flames and the water was afire."

Captain F. A. Gower of Fall River, master mariner and representing the owners of the *Pinthis,* expressed the opinion that the prow of the *Fairfax* plowed through the bulkhead of the *Pinthis* and that the damage on the port side of the *Fairfax* was due to her striking the engines of the tanker. He said there were between 11,500 and 12,000 barrels of oil and gasoline aboard the *Pinthis* when she left Fall River, intending to discharge half her cargo at Portland, Maine, and the balance at Chelsea, Massachusetts.

Captain Gower attributed the fire to a spark caused by the steel prow of the *Fairfax* plunging through the tanker's steel sides, followed by the ignition of oil and gasoline after the *Fairfax* went through the bulkhead that separated the tanks from parts of the vessel where there was fire. He discounted the theory that the oil and gasoline reached the boilers of the auxiliary engines on deck.

Acting on orders from Washington, Howard Wilcox, commander of the Provincetown Coast Guard area, which includes the stations at Brant Rock and North Scituate, later investigated charges that the men in charge of the stations were indefensibly lax in their duty in not sending boats out to rescue survivors of the *Fairfax-Pinthis* crash.

He queried Boatswain's Mate James McIntyre, who was in command of the North Scituate station. McIntyre, who had spent many years in the Coast Guard service, insisted that they could not begin any rescue movement until they received a "definite signal of distress" or were ordered by district officers. He defended his inaction by saying that he had talked by telephone with the Provincetown and Boston offices of the Coast Guard and had not received orders. Despite the fact that six reporters were at his station and newspaper offices were continually calling him to find whether he had started a boat toward the scene, McIntyre said that until he read the morning newspapers the crash was "just a rumor" to him.

Harbormaster Gerald Dwyer and James L. Rothery, a well-known resident of Scituate, were bitter in their denunciation of the Coast Guard for not helping those attempting to swim through the burning oil. They sent a telegram to Congressman Charles L. Gifford demanding a "full investigation." The telegram said:

> In view of the revelations made by newspaper investigation, we believe a full investigation of North Scituate Coast Guard is called for. The incompetency and inefficiency of the official life saving agency of the United States has been bared by fact that patrol boat 2360 did not proceed to disaster 10 miles away, although Coast Guard station knew of disaster before midnight. Two lives and perhaps more might have been saved if crew had acted within reasonable time and not waited until 5 o'clock Wednesday to proceed to scene of wreck.

Rear Admiral Frederick C. Bullard, commandant of the Coast Guard, immediately ordered Commander Wilcox to start an investigation and to give the press all the facts. Commander Wilcox, questioned at the Manomet station, gave out this statement:

The district commander had no information whatever of the disaster until he heard it over the radio at 8:05 A.M. (Wednesday), twelve hours after the collision. The radio said all passengers had been transferred to the steamer *Gloucester* and that the passengers had been landed at Boston. There was no information that any of the passengers had left the *Fairfax* in small boats at the time of the collision. Had there been a call for assistance sent out and the definite position of the collision given at least four boats from stations in the vicinity, North Scituate, Brant Rock, Gurnet, and Manomet Point, could have reached the scene in ninety minutes or less.

Bosn's Mate McIntyre, who was in charge at North Scituate station, received calls from several Boston newspapers late on the night of the collision. Nothing definite could be learned as to where the two ships came together. The newspapers that called stated that there was a report in Boston that there had been a collision at sea. No authority was given for the statement, merely that the collision was "off Scituate."

McIntyre did not want to go because he had no definite information and he deemed it best to wait for this information as to position. At no time did the station receive any word of the collision from a steamship or steamship company.

About 4 A.M. Wednesday McIntyre received a call from a Boston paper stating the *Fairfax* was in a collision somewhere off Scituate. Lacking information as to position, McIntyre waited until 4 P.M. that day until the fog lifted and then went out in a picket boat with a crew and searched from 4 to 10 P.M.

The course of the boat was north and south from Minot's light to the mouth of the North river, approximately six miles offshore. All they found was an expanse of oil burning near gas buoy No. 4, approximately twelve miles southeast of Scituate.

No wreckage was sighted. Observation was one to two miles, and the only things they sighted were two fishing boats. The search continued Thursday. The nearest station to the accident was Brant Rock, approximately eight miles from the scene. This station had no information of the disaster until the next morning when the crew heard it over the radio.

Later, at North Scituate Station, Bosn's Mate McIntyre admitted to newspapermen that absolutely no attempt was made to ascertain the position of the wreck following the calls from the Boston newspapers. He had two surf boats at his command, in addition to a motorboat usually used for rum patrol duty. When asked why he had not used this motorboat, he said it was used exclusively for rum patrol duty.

"If anything happened while we were trying to find the wreck," he said, "we'd get the devil for being away from our station." He declined to give his reasons for waiting until the fog lifted, when newspapermen, chartering a fishing boat, left early in the morning, hours before he attempted to get to the scene. When pressed for a definite reason for not ordering his crew of ten men into boats, McIntyre said, "We didn't go because we didn't feel like it."

He later said that survivors in the water "might have been struck by us, run into, ground up by our propeller. One couldn't see out there. Any survivors might have been man-gled."

Wreckage from the *Pinthis* eventually drifted ashore on Hen Island near the mouth of the North River in Marshfield, but the submerged fire on the bottom of the sea near what is now H buoy burned for seven days and seven nights before going out.

Scuba divers in 1974 visited the *Pinthis* hull but never reported on their findings.

All that I shall or should say concerning the *Fairfax-Pinthis* disaster has been recorded in this chapter. It is the task and privilege of the reader to make his own conclusions as to who should have done what and when.

Those who experienced and survived the holocaust of June 10, 1930, will never forget the terror they endured in the inferno of blazing oil that surrounded them that frightful night.

CHAPTER 2

THE LOSS OF THE *ROYAL TAR*

During the summer of 1836, a circus and menagerie toured the Canadian province of New Brunswick. At the close of a successful season the entire circus embarked on the *Royal Tar,* a steamer bound from Saint John Harbor, New Brunswick, to Portland, Maine. It was a new vessel built at Saint John that spring and named the *Royal Tar* because of King William IV's deep interest in the British navy.

Captain Thomas Reed was in command of the *Royal Tar* as she sailed out of Saint John Harbor on Friday, October 21, 1836, with her strange cargo of assorted animals, which included horses, two camels, Mogul the elephant, two lions, one Royal Bengal tiger, a gnu, and two pelicans. The circus brass band was also on board.

When the steamer began her voyage that Friday morning, the weather had been fine in every respect, but before the sun set a high westerly wind started to blow. The wind continued several days and forced the *Royal Tar* to seek shelter in Eastport Harbor, Maine, where she remained until the following Tuesday afternoon. Shortly after she left Eastport, rising winds again forced her to seek shelter, this time behind Fox Island. While the vessel was anchored about two miles off Fox Island Thoroughfare, the order was given to fill the ship's boilers.

Evidently the water in the boilers was much lower than had been believed, for when the pilot's son tested the lower cock he found it dry. The boy told his father, who mentioned the fact to Mr. Marshall, the second engineer in charge. Both father and son were informed that they were mistaken in believing the boilers dry, as everything was in order. However, it was the engineer who was in error, for a few minutes after the discussion, the boiler—empty—became red hot, setting fire to two wedges supporting the elephant stall. The fire gained headway rapidly, and by the time Captain Reed looked down the grating, the flames were beyond control. Realizing that the *Royal Tar* was doomed, he ordered the men to slip anchor, hoist a distress signal, and lower the boats. (It was later learned that the regular engineer had been up all night working on the boilers. Tired, he had entrusted his position to the second engineer, who in turn had given the task of watering the boilers to the fireman—and the fireman had not done it.)

Captain Reed took charge of the stern boat and came alongside the *Royal Tar,* where two able men, Mr. Sherwood and Mr. Fowler, joined him.

Sixteen other men jumped into the longboat, cut the ropes to drop their craft into the water, and started for shore. The strong wind rapidly swept them leeward in the direction of land, which they reached safely four hours later.

A revenue cutter, the *Veto,* was seen in the distance, approaching rapidly. When the cutter drew near, Captain Reed ordered his men to row over to her where she lay to windward. The men refused, infuriating Captain Reed.

"If any man refuses to run for the cutter, I'll throw him overboard," the captain threatened. The boat then made for the cutter, where the passengers received treatment.

The revenue cutter's pilot arrived near the *Royal Tar* with the *Veto*'s gig, but the flames of the burning vessel so frightened him that he dared not approach closely enough to effect the rescue of anyone. Passing around in back of the stern, the pilot saw passengers and members of the crew clinging to the ropes hanging over the sides. Terrified by their cries for help, he lost his nerve and steered back to the cutter without saving a single person. The cutter itself, with a heavy deckload of gunpowder, was unable to approach any closer to the burning steamer.

Working desperately to construct a substantial raft from the deck boards of the *Royal Tar,* a group of men aboard the burning ship managed to launch a makeshift float that supported them fairly well. However, just as they were about to push off from the vessel, the huge form of the elephant loomed directly over them, balanced for a terrifying moment at the taffrail, and smashed down through the air to land on the raft, sinking the float and drowning the men. The body of the elephant was found floating a few days later near Brimstone Island. It was said that every animal belonging to the menagerie was lost. Other accounts mention that when the horses jumped overboard they swam round and round the burning vessel until they sank, instead of making for shore where they might have been saved.

As the regular captain was not aboard, Captain Reed took charge of the revenue cutter. He steered the cutter in closer to the *Royal Tar* and then went across in a boat for those still left on board. By this time some of the passengers on the wreck had been hanging to ropes in the water for almost two hours. One by one the ropes would burn through, dropping the victims into the sea to their death.

One of the passengers, Mr. H. H. Fuller, clung to a rope over the stern until his strength failed him; then he twisted the line around his neck to prevent slipping into the sea. Four others, desperate to hold themselves above water, grabbed hold of his body, causing terrific pressure on his throat. Lifting his leg high out of water, in some way Fuller transferred the rope from his neck to his leg. A woman grabbed hold of his other leg and clung desperately to him. They were still in this awkward position when rescued a short time later.

Of the ninety-three persons on board, thirty-two passengers and members of the crew perished. One of the most unusual deaths was that of a man who lashed his small trunk to a plank, which he slid off into the sea successfully. Then he fastened a money belt containing $500 in silver around his waist, mounted the taffrail, and leaped into the sea. He did not realize the significant weight of the $500 in silver! He plummeted down through the waves and never rose to the surface again.

The passengers were high in their praise of the acts of Captain Reed, who did much to reduce the loss of life aboard the *Royal Tar*. One of the prominent passengers on board was quoted as follows:

> Captain Reed took charge of the stern boat, with two men, and kept her off the steamboat, which was a very fortunate circumstance, as it was the means of saving from 40 to 50 persons, and to him all credit is due for his deliberate and manly perseverance throughout the whole calamity.

> It is impossible to describe the appalling spectacle which the whole scene presented—the boat wrapped in flames, with nearly 100 souls on board, without any hope of relief, rending the air with their shrieks for help; the caravan of wild beasts on deck, ready to tear to pieces all that might escape the flames.

Shortly before sunset the last rescue boat, with a single survivor on board, left the *Royal Tar*. The passenger was a woman who had seen her sister and daughter perish before her eyes. After taking the unfortunate woman aboard, the revenue cutter started for the Isle of Haut to land the survivors. There the passengers obtained a schooner to take them to Portland, while the master and crew went to Eastport on another vessel.

On November 3, 1836, Captain Reed was presented with a purse of $700 for his heroic work during the fire. A few years later he was appointed harbormaster at Saint John. He became a picturesque figure around the Saint John waterfront, where he was often seen with his faithful dog walking at his side.

CHAPTER 3

THE WALKER EXPEDITION

One of the most awesome tales of the North Atlantic is so little known that I never met any person who could tell me the complete story of the catastrophe, although more than two centuries and a half ago it shocked the entire English-speaking world.

I first learned of this terrible multiple shipwreck in 1935 when I was preparing my book on Boston Harbor. Miss Carolyn E. Jakemann was assisting me at Harvard's Houghton Library when I came across Sir Hovendon Walker's journal of his expedition against Quebec, written in the year 1720. I could not resist digging into the pages of this fascinating account.

The reader may recall that Sir William Phips, who at one time found more than a million dollars in the sea, was not quite so fortunate when he made the first attempt to capture Quebec in 1690. Phips returned to Boston in defeat after over a thousand of his men had drowned and thirty-eight ships had been lost. The English smarted under this defeat for some years, and then in 1708 prepared another expedition. General McCartney planned to lead his troops against Quebec that year, but then took his regiments to Portugal instead. The Quebec expedition was not revived again until three more years had elapsed.

England was at war with France and Spain in the War of the Spanish Succession, fought from 1702 to 1713 and sometimes called Queen Anne's War. On April 11, 1711, Queen Anne, who dreamed of achieving naval successes to match the sweeping land victories of her dazzling army leader Marlborough, called Sir Hovendon Walker and General John Hill into her palace at St. James and handed Walker sealed orders, which she told him to open after he had sailed for Boston.

On April 29 Admiral Walker and his English fleet sailed from Great Britain. Upon opening his orders at sea, he learned of the details for the assault on Quebec. There followed a long, trying period of minor disappointments and mishaps, but Walker was determined to carry out his royal mission. He dreamed of winning a greater victory against the French at Quebec than that won by Sir Francis Drake against the Spanish Armada in 1588.

Walker's fleet reached Massachusetts Bay on June 24, and the flagship *Edgar* soon sighted the beacon on Boston's Great Brewster Island. Sixty-one ships, the largest fleet that had ever entered Boston Harbor, anchored in the roadstead.* Two impressive reviews under General Hill were later staged on Noddle's Island by picked regiments of Marlborough's finest soldiers.

Although eager to succeed in his mission, Walker had not underestimated the dangers ahead. After much effort he secured Captain Phips' original journal of the disastrous 1690 expedition against Quebec. Thus fortified, he laid plans care-

---

* The scene is depicted in a combination map and illustration of the period.

fully so he would not duplicate the treasure finder's failure. In fact, everything was done to make the capture of Quebec an easy conquest.

After the final parade on Noddle's Island was concluded and almost every soldier, sailor, and passenger was at last aboard his assigned vessel—a substantial number of deserters remained in Boston—the fleet sailed from Nantasket Road, Boston Harbor on July 30. Aboard the sixty-one transports and men-of-war were 9,385 men, with hundreds of women and children as well. The confident English leaders, not even considering the possibility of defeat this time, had made plans for the soldiers and their families to be quartered in the conquered citadel at Quebec.

Off Cape Breton, the lookouts on the flagship sighted a small French transport, the *Neptune,* on which a French captain named Paradis was transporting reinforcements for the very Quebec garrison that Admiral Walker would have to overcome before he subdued the French city. The Admiral delegated Captain Matthews of the *Chester* to withdraw from formation and capture the *Neptune,* which Matthews did handily.

When brought before Admiral Walker, the French captain proved ready and willing to answer the questions the anxious Admiral fired at him. His tongue loosened by payment of five hundred pistoles, Paradis told Walker many important facts concerning Saint Lawrence Bay, through the waters of which he had successfully completed forty trips. He then talked in great detail about the dangers of the Labrador Coast. In fact, Captain Paradis made such an impression on Admiral Walker that the Englishman decided Paradis could pilot the entire expedition, in spite of the fact that several Boston pilots, including the eminent John Bonner, had been brought along for precisely that purpose. How much the French cap-

tain, as pilot, was to blame for the events that followed is
a matter of conjecture.

Paradis did not minimize the perils of navigating the Gulf
of Saint Lawrence. Walker's Journal mentions his telling the
Englishmen that there were possible dangers ahead that might
leave "brave men famishing with hunger, drawing lots to see
who should die first to feed the rest." It was often true, according to the talkative French sea captain, that men "were
left dead in the march and frozen into statues for their own
monuments." If Paradis hoped by this discouraging talk to
make the Admiral turn back, he failed.

On August 16, 1711, while off Cape Gaspé, the flagship
Edgar sighted Bonaventure Island. The fleet continued on up
Gaspé Passage. Walker, carried away by his ambitious plans,
made tentative arrangements to secure his ships at Quebec
for the winter. Several of the men-of-war were dispatched to
destroy the fishing fleet at Bonaventure Island, but a dead
calm prevented this action. They did reach Gaspé Harbor,
however, and burned a fishing craft and several fishermen's
dories there. A dozen or so huts were also set afire.

By this time Admiral Walker's worries were many. The
various craft of the fleet seemed to be scattering, and he felt
it necessary to issue definite orders for procedure:

> No commodore is to suffer any ship of his division to
> go ahead of him, and in case any do, to fire at them;
> and the men-of-war in his division, or next to that ship
> that goes ahead, shall make up sail to get up with her
> and cause that shot to be paid for by the master.

Shortly afterward a stiff breeze pushed the mighty fleet up
through the Gaspé Passage and toward the shores of Labrador at a rate much faster than Paradis appeared to think

possible. And so it was that at ten o'clock on the night of August 22, 1711, in foggy rough weather, over forty miles beyond the point where Paradis had indicated they were, the fleet entered an area of extreme danger. Before they realized what was happening, one after another of the vessels smashed into Egg Island. Eight great transports were ripped apart on the rocks and broke into fragments. It was a scene of great confusion as the other ships of the fleet attempted to sail away from the dangerous island. The men-of-war all escaped, but the eight transports that were shipwrecked carried over 1300 officers, soldiers, and seamen to their deaths, together with an appalling number of the men's families, the actual count of which will never be ascertained.

The transports that piled ashore were the *Marlborough, Smyrna Merchant, Chatham, Content, Colchester, Isabella and Catherine, Nathanial and Elizabeth*, and the *Samuel and Alice*.

In this mighty disaster, the Windrasse and the Seymour Regiments, together with two complete companies of the Royal Guards, identified by their scarlet coats, were entirely wiped out. At least 1342 men drowned, and their families numbered hundreds more.

Admiral Hovendon Walker was simply overwhelmed by the disaster, and on August 25, 1711, he brought together as many ships as possible for a conference of their captains. Here are the details of that conference in the St. Lawrence River, in the very words recorded at that time:

The following Minutes were taken by Mr. Gordon, *General Hill's Secretary.*

Minutes taken at a Consultation of Sea Officers in the River of *St. Laurence*, the 25th of *Aug.* 1711. abord her Majesty's Ship the *Windsor*.

Present
Sir Hovenden Walker Knt. Rear-Admiral of the White, etc.

Captain		of the	
	Soans		*Swiftsure.*
	Mitchel		*Monmouth.*
	Arris		*Windsor.*
	Walton		*Mountague.*
	Gore		*Dunkirk.*
	Paddon		*Edgar.*
	Cockburn		*Sunderland.*
	Rouse		*Saphire.*

The Admiral told these Gentlemen that he had called them together, to ask their Advice what was now to be done in the present Juncture of our Affairs; that we had lost many Transports, with a great Number of Men in the Entrance of the said River.

Several of the Captains said, that they not having been sooner consulted touching the Navigation of the River, could not now determine.

The Admiral said, that the Pilots, *viz. Paradis* and *Bonner,* had been consulted, and did agree in their Opinions, in what was done; but the Question was now, What was to be done? and if there was any thing wrong in his Conduct, he seemed to hint he was to answer it in another Place. And then he desired their Answer to this short Question, whether it was practicable to go up the River *St. Laurence* as far as *Quebec,* with the Men of War and Transports or not.

Captain *Mitchel* said, his Pilot had told him the 22d of this Month, that we steer'd too far Northerly.

All the Captains did agree that the Pilots were very ignorant, and not to be depended upon.

The conference came to an end. Although hopelessly stunned by the enormity of the catastrophe, Walker ordered Captain Cook of the *Leonard*, and other masters to cruise in the vicinity in an attempt to save life and property, while the captain of his flagship, the *Edgar*, did likewise.

It is true that the various craft of the squadron sailed briefly about the waters around Egg Island, supposedly on the alert for survivors. What Admiral Walker never found out, however, was that had they been more thorough, the sailors could have rescued scores of officers, men, women, and children who were still alive, either on the island or on the Labrador mainland. If they had gone ashore and organized search parties instead of confining their efforts merely to sailing around the bays and inlets, they could have saved scores upon scores of lives.

Several hundred of the survivors had floated ashore to the mainland on fragments of wreckage. Having lived through the catastrophe of the shipwreck, they set out bravely for help, poorly clothed and with no way of obtaining provisions. However the early winter caught them before they could get very far, and their footprints in the snow, found later, led for miles into the interior of Labrador. Some of the unfortunates had secreted themselves in hollow trees for warmth; others had sought protection under piles of hay and wild herbs; but all perished sooner or later, and their bodies were eventually discovered by the natives.

Mère Juchereau, writing of the French who visited the island the following fall, tells of the way in which the people of Quebec learned of the disaster. It was not until October 19, 1711, almost two months later, that they heard of the shipwrecks at Egg Island and the proposed British invasion of their city. It was Monsieur de la Valtrie, returning to Quebec from Labrador, who brought the first news. When the joyous tidings of deliverance from the hated English fleet became known, the entire populace poured out into the streets. To commemorate this second escape from the British in twenty-one years, the name of the small church in the lower town, already known as *Notre Dame de la Victorie,* was changed to *Notre Dames des Victoires.* Everyone at Quebec spoke of the miracle that had saved their city, and more than a hundred poems were written of the glorious shipwrecks that had prevented the English from capturing them.

Five ships were outfitted at once from Quebec, with forty men, a pastor, and provisions, to winter at Egg Island. There they planned to salvage as much property as possible from the shipwrecks. Those who spent that winter on the island saw sights terrible to behold. By actual count over two thousand naked men, women and children from the stricken vessels were strewn along the shores. Some of the dead bodies looked as though they were gnashing their teeth; others seemed to be tearing out their hair; a few were joined in final embrace. One group of seven women was discovered with their hands locked in a fatal circle.

The spoils from the wrecks were many. Heavy anchors, chains, cannon balls, guns, plate, bells, rigging, and every type of ironware were brought up to Quebec. In a few days over $20,000 worth of material had been obtained as souvenirs of the "British Armada," and later another $50,000 worth of spoils was brought from the island.

Two days after the shipwrecks the survivors of the British fleet held a council of war. Captain John Bonner of Boston spoke out plainly to the effect that pilots of worth had never been consulted at any time during the trip, implying that in any case the French Captain Paradis should not have been trusted.

Additional grief awaited Sir Hovendon Walker when he reached England. Leaving the *Edgar* at Portsmouth after the remainder of the expedition's forces had returned home, he arrived in London only to learn that the *Edgar* had blown up, with all aboard lost! His account follows:

October 16. Being come to *London*, soon after I received a Letter from *Portsmouth*, with the melancholy *News* of the *Edgar's* being blown up; whereby as to my own particular, I sustain'd a very considerable Loss, my Household Goods, Stores, and most of my Publick Papers, Books, Draughts of *Quebec* River, Journals, Charts, Sir *William Phips* Journal of his *Canada* Expedition, all the Officers original Demands, Supplies and Receipts, my own contingent Accounts, with several other Papers of Consequence.

In the Evening I waited upon Mr. Secretary *St. John*, who seemed very much concern'd at the Disappointment of the Expedition.

17. This Forenoon I waited upon the Admiralty, where was an account of the *Edgar's* being blown up and not one Man saved.

19. I came to *Windsor* last Night, and this Morning was introduced by his Grace the Duke of *Shrewsbury* Lord Chamberlain, to the Queen: Her Majesty was pleased to receive me very graciously, and told me when I kiss'd Her Hand, She was glad to see me. I said, I was very sorry my Power to serve Her Majesty in the late Expedition, had not been equal to my Zeal, and mention'd the great Loss I had by the *Edgar's* being blown up.

When I returned to *London*, I apply'd myself to the obtaining the Bills to be paid that had been drawn from *Boston*, and to get my own contingent Accounts pass'd.

But other blows were to fall. Ridiculed and abused, Hovendon Walker was practically chased out of London by his former associates, the Lords of the Admiralty. He finally found the humiliation too great and sailed for America.

During his declining years he spent much of his time reading the works of the ancient Roman poet Horace, finding serenity in Horace's admonitions concerning action in the face of adversity.

"Show yourself brave and undaunted in the face of adversity," Horace said. "Also if you are wise, you will furl your swelling sail, though the wind seem too favorable for it."

Horace's words gave Walker peace and tranquility during the remaining period of his career, in which he spent many hours writing his journal. Published in 1720, the lengthy volume defended his actions, quoting Horace's words which are translated above:

REBUS ANGUSTIS ANIMOSUS ATQUE FORTIS APPARE: SAP-
IENTER IDEM CONTRAHES VENTO NIMIUM SECUNDO TUR-
GIDA VELA

CHAPTER 4

THE STORM OF OCTOBER 1804

One of the outstanding October gales of all times swept across New England on the morning of October 9, 1804. The tempest brought heavy rain in the southern part of New England, while the people in Massachusetts and to the north experienced a snowstorm. First the wind blew from the southeast, and then early in the afternoon it veered to the north northeast, increasing in intensity until sunset, when its terrific force blew down houses, barns, trees, and hundreds of chimneys. Before midnight the worst of the gale had passed, although the snow and wind continued for two days.

It was one of the worst October storms ever witnessed in Massachusetts, with snowfall averaging from five to fourteen inches. At Concord, New Hampshire, the snow was two feet deep, but in Vermont only five inches fell. Farmers were among the worst sufferers. Fruit orchards were blown down everywhere. Cattle and sheep died by the hundreds, and thousands of fowl perished. At Thomaston, Maine, a sixty-acre timber lot was almost completely blown down. Such great sections of timber were destroyed that entirely new views were possible; houses and other buildings never before visible from a distance could be seen across valleys and townships.

The change was so pronounced in certain sections that the surroundings seemed to have become entirely different. People felt that they were in a strange place.

In Massachusetts the South Church in Danvers lost its roof, while in Peabody over 30,000 unburned bricks were ruined by the gale. The spire of the Beverly meeting house broke off.

In Boston, the wind blew the battlements from a new building onto the roof of a residence occupied by Ebenezer Eaton, who had left his house just in time. Four others were caught in the ruins, one dying later. The roof was ripped off King's Chapel and dropped to the ground two hundred feet away. The handsome steeple of the Old North Church was toppled into the street, landing partly on a building nearby and demolishing it. No one was inside. The buildings over Paul Revere's copper furnaces were destroyed.

Shipping in the harbor suffered considerably, with several persons losing their lives. The schooner *Dove* was wrecked on Ipswich Bar, all seven on board perishing. The sloops *Hannah* and *Mary* were driven on the beach at Cohasset at about the same time. Captain Gardner of the *Hannah* was swept off the deck and drowned, but the others aboard were saved. The crew from the *Mary* were successful in reaching shore alive. The ship *Protector*, with a cargo valued at $100,-000, was wrecked on Cape Cod five miles south of Cape Cod Light. Only one man was lost.

The Reverend William Bentley of Salem said that this gale was the heaviest blow ever known in that town. He recorded the storm in his diary as follows:

9. This morning the wind was in the South & the weather uncertain. About 7 it shut down & it began to rain at S.E. & soon the wind rose & the wind changed to N.E. Its violence increased till sundown & continued all night. The barn belonging to Perkins on the Neck,

was blown down & one horse killed. Beckets barn down, all the vessels drove from their anchors. Chimnies were blown down, roof & windows injuried & trees destroyed in great number.

The fences suffered so much that in the eastern part of the Town which I visited it was easy to pass over any lot in that part of the Town. The damage is so equally divided that few have special cause to complain. It was the heaviest blow ever known in Salem & it will be remembered as the Violent Storm of 9 Oct. 1804. We had thunder & lightning all day. We lost the Railing from the top of the house in which I live. It was totally destroyed.

10. We are every moment receiving accounts of the injuries done by the Storm. The Vessels in Cape Ann & Marblehead that were at anchor are ashore. The damage done in Boston is great. The celebrated Steeple of the North Church is blown down. Mr. Atwater Phippen who for many years has noticed the fall of rain, distinguished the rain of yesterday as the greatest he ever knew, four inches fell in the day & three inches in the night.

11. Continued account of the Storm. From the Coast, accounts general only as yet. Roads everywhere much obstructed by the fall of trees, &c. Revere's Buildings over his furnace destroyed. Not of great value. Covering of Chapel Church tower blown down. Mr. Eaton at Boston, new brick walls tumbled upon his old house from which he had just time to escape. The woman who lived with him killed, servants wounded.

The spire of Charleston steeple bent down. The top of Beverly steeple blown off. The dome of the Tabernacle in this town uncapped, & shattered & Lantern. A Vessel from Cape Ann harbour, belonging to Kennebunk, lost her anchor & split her sails & drove up over our Bar into the Cove within the Beacon upon Ram Horn rock. This is the only Vessel ashore on our coast not in the Harbour. The Boston account is an almost total destruction of all small boats at the wharves. The damage to Houses, buildings, trees, fences, &c. is incalculable, but such losses not heavy to individuals, but a distressing loss to the public.

12. This day I rode through south fields & Marblehead farms to Nahant. Every where trees are blown down & barns unroofed & the road in several places would have been impassable had it not been cleared. Even at Nahant Great head, Wood lost part of the roof of his new Barn erected this year.

The reports are endless, but we cannot distinguish truth from falsehood at any distance from home at present. But the reports shew the state of the public mind. The quantity of seaweed driven up is beyond any former example. I had a good opportunity of examining a rich variety on every part of Nahant. The most common there in deep water is the Kelp, the seagrass & the wrack as they are called. The *Dulce Conpici,* &c. were in less abundance. It would not have been imagined that the beaches over which we passed had ever been used for pleasure had they been seen only after the late storm.

13. I cannot refuse to adopt the belief that the late storm was the most severe ever felt in this part of America. All the accounts which I have seen represent nothing like it. In Boston, the old people are said to represent that a storm like it happened 16 September 1727. As yet I have found no tradition of such a storm among our old people or upon record or any report of its consequences. I suspect as our winters have less horrour we partake more of a southern climate from the great quantity of heat & consequently have more stormy weather of this kind & therefore may expect more of it in future

years. I can find no history of wharves, ships, trees, houses, fences, out houses which lead to suspect great calamities from high winds.

From Cape Ann we learn that many of their boats were lost entirely & some greatly injuried by the storm. But we have hopes from the news from Plymouth & Portland, that the storm was much more limited than we have expected from its great severity here & near Boston.

CHAPTER 5

~~~~~~~~~~~

THE *NANCY*

A substantial number of present-day residents of Massachusetts can recall the year 1927, when the five-masted schooner *Nancy* was stranded in the same storm that brought death to eight members of the Coast Guard rum chaser *CG 238* off Cape Cod, a tale I relate elsewhere in this book. Just as people numbered the years after the great Boston Fire of 1872, then later after the Chelsea Fire of 1908, so it has come to be that many now alive enjoy figuring out how many years have passed since the *Nancy* came ashore at Nantasket Beach.

The story of the *Nancy* is one of the sagas of New England maritime history. It all began on February 19, 1927, when the *Nancy* anchored off Boston Light to ride out an expected gale or blizzard.

Captain E. M. Baird of Floral Park, Long Island, New York, had sailed the *Nancy* away from Nickerson Wharf in South Boston late in the afternoon of February 18, but on reaching the Boston Lightship he decided to find out what the weather ahead might be. He turned on his five-tube radio set and learned that a storm was on the way. Interviewed on February 20 at the Point Allerton Coast Guard Station, he told this story:

"I decided it was best to drop our anchors near sight of the lightship. There was a strong wind, but our big and little anchors made us safe until afternoon. Yesterday at noon believed that the storm was abating. The barometer was at 30:15 all morning long and began to go down at the time we lost our big anchor. The chain parted about 2:30 P.M Immediately the flag was hoisted, union down, but no one noticed that we were in distress.

"Then for about three hours all aboard worked like beavers hauling in about ninety fathoms, preparatory to putting on a reserve anchor, and after this was done the distress flag was pulled down again for the time being.

"After dark the storm had grown so desperate that we became alarmed. We would have liked to have had a cutter then, but try as we did, our signals to the lightship received no response. Apparently they had no means of communication with the mainland, and so we had to suffer out the night few of the men getting any sleep.

"Everything went along O.K. until the chain on our starboard anchor parted again at 7:30 this morning, although throughout the night I was afraid that we were going to be carried into Harding's Ledge. But we escaped that fate, only to avert it again by the narrowest of margins when the chain parted about one o'clock this afternoon, and then all three of our anchors had dropped into the sea.

"There was easily a seventy-five knot gale whipping up the seas as the chain parted the third time. The water was drifting like snow in the howling wind, and it was necessary to raise the staysail, a jib next to the foremast, to steer us clear of Harding's Ledge off Nantasket.

"For a time it really looked as though we would be dashed to pieces on the ledge, but I worked hard and managed to bring her up here on the beach. I should say that we were within two hundred yards of Harding's Ledge, when knowing of the clean stretch of beach here, I decided to steer for this place, as I knew that we would not be damaged too much.

"I have been sailing the seas for thirty-three years, and this is my first experience of being beached. I have been in some very tough storms during those years, but yesterday's was as tough as any I have ever encountered," were his concluding remarks to those of us who listened to him at the Point Allerton Coast Guard Station.

As she fought her losing battle, the huge five-master came slowly in, her great hulk constantly battered by towering waves that fell over each other in endless profusion. Captain Baird watched the giant billows as the *Nancy* drove her keel on the shore. The wind filled the air with biting sand, and the surf pounded relentlessly as the schooner neared the end of her voyage.

With the bellying skysail tugging at the bolt rope, the five-masted craft drove high on the beach at Surfside, Hull. Ned Blossom, patrolman at Surfside, was the nearest to the oncoming *Nancy*, and he telephoned to the Hull police station. A volunteer crew of rescuers was quickly rounded up.

The men rolled out the surfboat of the Massachusetts Humane Society. A truck mounting a snowplow pulled the surfboat across to a position opposite to where the *Nancy* was pounding ashore. Driven diagonally toward the shelving beach, the ship had her starboard bow closest to the shore.

It was then high tide, with about a hundred and eighty yards separating the *Nancy* from the railroad tracks. Even then a few hardy souls were on the shore, with the sleet and sand driving against them, but when word reached the townspeople of Hull, crowds soon began to congregate.

There has always been controversy as to which residents and coast guardsmen of Hull assisted in the rescue of the crew of the *Nancy*. No one knows how it started, but it can never be settled, as several of those claiming participation in the actual rescue effort are now dead. The story below is as close as we can come to the truth in 1976, almost half a century after the incident.

As the men ashore watched the *Nancy* successfully avoid hitting Harding's Ledge, they prepared for the eventual beaching of the great schooner.

Captain Osceola F. James of Center Hill organized the lifeboat crew, which consisted of Captain Adelbert Nickerson of the Nantasket steamer *Mayflower*, formerly of the Point Allerton Coast Guard Station, Captain Edward Hatch, John Sullivan, Louis Hurley, Robert Blossom, Clifton Jaeger, Burgess Ruderham, and Joseph James.

Another crew arrived by automobile. Organized under the leadership of Coast Guard Captain Ralph C. Rich, they started for the breeches buoy and the gun, although they soon found that neither was necessary.

Soon the lifeboat was launched into the breakers. It was drawn up under the *Nancy's* starboard rope ladder, where the crew members caught suitcases and dunnage dropped from above. Boatswain Alexander Holmberg of Brooklyn, carrying the ship's mascot, a black cat, was the first to reach the surfboat. The others were Captain Baird; Engineer Charles M. Rathburn, New York; Steward S. A. White, Norfolk; Carlin Burrell, Lynn; Ruby Hatfield, Revere; Frank Combs, Charlestown; and Carl Michaelson, Norfolk.

There were several exciting moments as the heavily laden lifeboat was rowed ashore, but the landing on Nantasket Beach was successful. Within an hour rescuers and rescued were enjoying coffee at the Coast Guard station.

For one of the *Nancy's* crew, Ruby Hatfield, it was his sixth mishap at sea. Previously he had been wrecked off Black Rock, Nova Scotia; again off Carr's Beach; still later stranded on Christmas Day at Beaver Harbor, New Brunsvick. On two other occasions Hatfield had abandoned sinking fishing schooners.

The *Nancy* did not break up, as many expected, and she became the goal of hundreds upon hundreds of sightseers from all over New England, as happened similarly in 1956, twenty-nine years later when the 441-foot Italian freighter *Etrusco* beached at Scituate. There was one great difference, however. No sightseers were able to get aboard the *Etrusco* because of her high sides and her position half in and half out of the water. In the case of the *Nancy,* a ramp was soon arranged for boarding, and payment of a relatively small fee allowed visitors who wished to board her to tour certain areas of the schooner.

Every so often during high runs of tides, efforts were made to float the *Nancy*, but as the years went by she became a fixture at Nantasket Beach. One day, when the tides were accompanied by a moderate storm, the five-masted schooner slipped a short distance toward the sea but grounded again. In another later gale she went up the beach ten feet higher than previously.

Finally it was agreed that she be broken up. Her towering masts were sold to the Hitchcock Quarry in Quincy. Residents of Hull took much of the lumber. Gradually her huge bulk disappeared from the beach, and the keel area was eventually buried in the sand. No one ever expected to see her again, but in the winter of 1940, during a nor'easter, the keel of the *Nancy* washed out of the sands at Nantasket Beach. The next storm buried her again. Without question, tons of her bottom and keel are still below the surface of the sands of Nantasket.

Built at Portland, Oregon, in 1918 for the French government, the *Nancy* had cost $650,000. Originally constructed as an auxiliary steam schooner, she was rebuilt for sailing in 1925, when she was sold to S. C. Forde of Philadelphia for the coal trade. Her gross registration was 2100 tons and her cargo tonnage totaled 3500.

Captain Baird had taken over command of the *Nancy* shortly before the last week in January, at Norfolk, Virginia, from which port he sailed the schooner to Boston with load of coal for South Boston.

Only a handful of residents witnessed the beaching of the *Nancy* at Nantasket, and of those few three are still alive today.* However, those who saw her and read about her through the years are many. They look back at her as an old friend associated with the glamour of the days of sail.

* Oliver Olson, Charles Short, and Louis Hurley.

CHAPTER 6

A STRANGE PREMONITION, OR THE LOSS OF THE RUM CHASER *CG 238*

On February 21, 1927, Mrs. Joseph Maxim of Westville Street, Dorchester, experienced a tragic dream concerning her boy Joseph. In the dream she saw her son, a Coast Guardsman aboard rum chaser *CG 238*, struggling for his life, after which she was approached by her sister, who told her to put on mourning clothes.

Mrs. Maxim awakened in a shaken state. Several hours later a messenger brought the news that her son was among those missing from the wreck of the *CG 238,* and word soon followed that he had drowned.

Actually, every member of the crew aboard the *CG 238* perished in what was the first trip her commander had ever made as officer-in-charge. All eight went to their deaths in the surging seas off Provincetown on Cape Cod.

Early the night before, on February 20, 1927, the 75-foot rum chaser had sent her first message of distress by the blinker system. Every Coast Guard station in the area was alerted, but a seventy-five-mile-an-hour gale and blinding snow blocked all attempts to save the eight men. The blizzard was possibly the worst since the steamer *Portland* sank in the storm of 1898. It had been in progress about thirty hours when the *CG 238* dropped two anchors about three miles off shore.

Highland Light crewman Clarence Carlos picked up the blinker message that the rum chaser was in distress, her engines broken down and her radio out of commission. The SOS message came immediately afterward.

Carlos notified his commanding officer, who informed other stations by telephone and radio of the *CG 238*'s peril. All night long the crews from three Coast Guard stations along the shore stood by, awaiting a possible lull in the storm, which never came. Every so often the lights of the *238* were sighted.

With the coming of dawn the wreck of the *CG 238* could be seen. She had hit the bar and broken in pieces. Bits of the wreckage washed up along the shore.

Later that day two bodies were sighted about halfway between Peaked Hill Station and Highland Light Station. A watch was found in the pocket of one man, the hands stopped at 4:57, indicating the time when the patrol craft began to break up. The remains were those of Boatswain's Mate Raymond H. Clark of Dorchester and Boatswain's Mate Charles H. Freeburn of Philadelphia. The other members of the crew were Boatswain Jesse K. Riberbank of Oak Bluffs, commander of the craft on his first trip; Chief Mechanic Cornelius Shea of Roxbury; mechanic Joseph Maxim; cook Clarence Alexander of South Carolina; coxswain Leo Kryzabowski; and Fred C. McCausland of Portland, Maine. A ninth regular member of the crew, Edward F. Cronin of Lynn, was a patient at the Chelsea Naval Hospital when the storm hit, and so escaped being a victim of the disaster.

Apparently the *CG 238* broke up shortly before five o'clock in the morning, but what happened in the twelve-hour inter-

al between the sending out of the first blinker message and
he actual destruction of the craft is a mystery that will never
be solved.

According to the surmise of Captain E. B. Andrews of the
Highland Light Coast Guard Station, the rum chaser had
been anchored until 2:30 in the morning, when she either
broke adrift or began dragging her anchor. She probably
passed over the outer bar and her anchors may have caught
again, to subject her to the giant breakers that battered her
to pieces.

Because of the tremendous surf, Captain Andrews could
not launch his surfboat for rescue work. The Lyle gun, which
sends a projectile a quarter mile or more to ships in distress,
could not reach the vessel, as she was then about a mile from
shore. At least four rescue craft were in the general vicinity,
including the revenue cutters *Tuscarora, Redwing, Pauling,*
and *Cummings,* but the *238* was in water too shallow for
their draft.

A statement that a coastal merchant steamer was within a
short distance of the *238* and did nothing to help has been
circulated, but what the captain of the steamer could have
done will never be known.

CHAPTER 7

THE *ACTIVE* AND THE *BETSY*

The meeting of the Casco Bay schooner *Active* and the Marblehead schooner *Betsy* took place off the white tower of Cape Cod's Highland Light and proved to have not only historical but literary significance as well.

At midnight on Friday, October 28, 1808, Keeper Isaac Small of Highland Light heard the sound of a gunshot some distance offshore from the lighthouse. Peering into the darkness, he was able to detect the source of the firing.

At that identical moment Captain Benjamin "Floyd" Ireson, who had been fishing off the Grand Banks, was sailing toward his home port of Marblehead aboard the schooner *Betsy*. He heard the same gun firing off Highland Light and found it to be a distress signal from the Brunswick, Maine, schooner *Active*, then sinking. He decided to give what assistance he could. However, the waves that night were mountainous, and the crew aboard the *Betsy* protested when the captain announced he would attempt to rescue the unfortunate sailors on the *Active*. Nevertheless, Ireson approached the foundering schooner and called encouragement to those aboard.

"We'll stand by," he shouted, but the sea was far too high to launch a dory. The *Betsy*'s crew became frightened and ebellious, urging the captain to sail for Marblehead, but he insisted upon waiting for the dawn to make a final rescue effort. After several hours of arguing, his sailors asserted their rights, claiming that they had been asked to do something beyond the usual call of duty of Marblehead fishermen, and Ireson finally gave in to their demands. However, after leaving the sinking vessel, the crewmen grew apprehensive about their reception when they arrived at Marblehead. They began to talk among themselves, stirring up false courage and blaming the captain for their own reluctance.

The *Betsy* reached port on Sunday, October 30. Ireson and his crew went to their respective homes after telling a brief story of their encounter with the sinking schooner. On hearing the news of a boat in distress, two different craft, manned by eager volunteers, left for her position off Highland Light. When they returned, they announced that they had found no signs of vessel or men. By this time the crew of the *Betsy* had let word circulate that Captain Ireson had been the one who was unwilling to wait around for dawn to attempt rescue work, while the captain maintained a stolid silence.

A day later the sloop *Swallow* sailed into Marblehead Harbor with four survivors from the *Active*, Captain Given—whose name is erroneously spelled Gibbons in some accounts—and three passengers. Given explained that the *Active* had sprung a leak at eleven o'clock that Friday night and that he had fired his distress gun shortly afterward. Then he related how Captain Ireson had brought the *Betsy* alongside and had called across to inquire if he could help, after which he had sailed away without giving any assistance.

Captain Given told how a Mr. Hardy of Truro had rowed out in a whaleboat, taking off the four who were saved, but that he was unable to rescue four other persons, who perished in the wreck when the storm returned with renewed fury that Saturday morning. Captain Given and his men had then been placed aboard the revenue cutter *Good Intent,* which sailed them across to Boston. From there the sloop *Swallow* took them over to Marblehead.

When the survivors were landed at Marblehead, a great feeling of resentment developed against Captain Ireson, whom people erroneously believed responsible for the loss of the four crew members aboard the *Active.* This antagonism was soon transformed into hostile action. A crowd went to Ireson's home. After causing a commotion outside his house they gained courage and entered his residence, where they manhandled him and pulled him outside. They had placed a dory in the street, and they bound him to the thwarts and tarred and feathered him.

Their next step was to drag the dory through the streets of Marblehead, with a great multitude of men and boys following and jeering. When the strange procession arrived at Workhouse Rocks, the bottom of the dory collapsed, and Captain Ireson finished his trip in a cart.

The parade was stopped on the outskirts of Salem by the residents there, and the men turned around and marched back into Marblehead, where Ireson was finally left at his own door. He had remained silent during the entire trip, but as he stood in his doorway he looked out over the assembled mob:

"I thank you for my ride, gentlemen," he remarked, "but you will live to regret it!"

Wondering just what he had implied, several leaders of the mob talked with the members of his crew. Explanations by the embarrassed sailors soon made the others realize that a great injustice had been done. An act of violence and shame had been perpetrated on an innocent man.

To the credit of the townspeople of Marblehead, it must be admitted that from that day on, they accepted Captain Ireson as a true citizen, who was blameless for his crew's reluctance to risk their lives.

Unfortunately, a native of Marblehead was later a classmate of poet John Greenleaf Whittier at Haverhill Academy. Whether Whittier's friend left Marblehead before learning the truth, or just did not care about the facts will never be known, but Whittier took account of the incident as the people of Marblehead originally thought it had happened, and composed therefrom his famous "Skipper Ireson's Ride," excerpts from which are quoted below:

> Of all the rides since the birth of time,
> Told in story or sung in rhyme,—
> On Apuleius's Golden Ass,
> Or one-eyed Calendar's horse of brass,
> Witch astride of a human hack,
> Islam's prophet on Al-Borák,—
> The strangest ride that ever was sped
> Was Ireson's, out from Marblehead!
> > Old Floyd Ireson, for his hard heart,
> > Tarred and feathered and carried in a cart
> > By the women of Marblehead!
>
> *   *   *
>
> Small pity for him!—He sailed away
> From a leaking ship in Chaleur Bay,—
> Sailed away from a sinking wreck,
> With his own townspeople on her deck!
> "Lay by! lay by!" they called to him:
> Back he answered, "Sink or swim!
> Brag of your catch of fish again!"
> And off he sailed through fog and rain!
> > Old Floyd Ireson, for his hard heart,
> > Tarred and feathered and carried in a cart
> > By the women of Marblehead!
> Fathoms deep in dark Chaleur
> That wreck shall lie for evermore.

Mother and sister, wife and maid,
Looked from the rocks of Marblehead
Over the moaning and rainy sea,—
Looked for the coming that might not be!
What did the winds and the sea-birds say
Of the cruel captain who sailed away?—
    Old Floyd Ireson, for his hard heart,
    Tarred and feathered and carried in a cart
    By the women of Marblehead!

*   *   *

Then the wife of the skipper lost at sea
Said, "God has touched him!–why should we?"
Said an old wife mourning her only son,
"Cut the rogue's tether and let him run!"
So with soft relentings and rude excuse,
Half scorn, half pity, they cut him loose,
And gave him a cloak to hide him in,
And left him alone with his shame and sin.
    Poor Floyd Ireson, for his hard heart,
    Tarred and feathered and carried in a cart
    By the women of Marblehead!

*   *   *

In 1880 Samuel Roads, Jr., writing in his *History and Traditions of Marblehead,* gave the true story of "Skipper Ireson's Ride." Roads tells of the arrival of the *Betsy* and Captain Ireson, and of the falsehoods spread by the crew. The account is essentially as I have narrated it above. Excerpts from the Roads tale follow:

The excitement and indignation of the people on the reception of this news can be better imagined than described. . . . On the following day, the sloop *Swallow* arrived having on board Captain Gibbons [Given] the master of the ill-fated schooner. He corroborated the story told by the crew of the *Betsey* and stated that the *Active* sprung a leak at about eleven o'clock on Friday night. An hour later the *Betsey* was spoken, "but contrary to the principles of humanity" she sailed away without giving any assistance. On Saturday Captain Gibbons [Given] and three of the passengers were taken off the wreck by Mr. Hardy of Truro, in a whaleboat. Four other persons were left on the wreck but the storm increased so rapidly that it was found impossible to return to their rescue. Captain Gibbons [Given] was placed on board the revenue cutter *Good Intent* and afterward on board the sloop *Swallow* in which he came to Marblehead.

This statement by one who had so narrowly escaped a watery grave made a deep impression on the fishermen and they determined to demonstrate their disapproval of Skipper Ireson's conduct by a signal act of vengeance. Accordingly on a bright moonlit night the unfortunate skipper was suddenly seized by several powerful men and securely bound. He was then placed in a dory and besmeared from head to feet with tar and feathers, was dragged through the town, escorted by a multitude of men and boys. When opposite the locality now known as Workhouse Rocks the bottom of the dory came out and the prisoner finished the remainder of his ride to Salem in a cart. . . .

When too late to make reparation for the wrong they had committed, the impulsive fishermen realized that they had perpetrated an act of the greatest injustice upon an innocent man.

Roads sent a copy to poet Whittier. After he read the story, Whittier wrote to Mr. Roads as follows:

> Oak Knoll, Danvers
> 5th Mo., 18, 1880

Samuel Roads, Jr.

My Dear Friend:—I heartily thank thee for a copy of thy "History of Marblehead." I have read it with great interest and think good use has been made of the abundant material.

No town in Essex County has a record more honorable than Marblehead; no one has done more to develop the industrial interest of our New England sea-board, and certainly none have given such evidence of self-sacrificing patriotism. I am glad the story of it has been at last told, and told so well. I have now no doubt that thy version of Skipper Ireson is a correct one. My verse was solely founded on a fragment of rhyme which I heard from one of my early schoolmates, a native of Marblehead.

I supposed the story to which it referred dated back at least a century. I knew nothing of the particulars, and the narrative of the ballad was pure fancy. I am glad for the sake of truth and justice that the real facts are given in thy book. I certainly would not knowingly do injustice to any one dead or living.

> I am truly, thy friend,
> JOHN G. WHITTIER.

New England poet Charles Timothy Brooks wrote a vigorous plea for the maligned captain, but mispelled Ireson's nickname.

> Old Flood Ireson! all too long
> Have jeer and jibe and ribald song

Done thy memory cruel wrong.
Old Flood Ireson sleeps in his grave;
Howls of a mad mob, worse than the wave,
Now no more in his ear shall rave!
Gone is the pack and gone the prey,
Yet old Flood Ireson's ghost today
Is hunted still down Time's highway.
Old wife Fame, with a fish horn's blare
Hooting and tooting the same old air,
Drags him along the thoroughfare.
Mocked evermore with the old refrain,
Skilfully wrought to a tuneful strain,
Jingling and jolting he comes again
Over the road of old renown,
Fair, broad avenue leading down
Through South Fields to Salem town.
Scourged and stung by the Muse's thong,
Mounted high on the car of song,
Sight that cries, O Lord! how long
Shall Heaven look on and not take part
With the poor old man and his fluttering heart,
Tarred and feathered and carried in a cart?
Old Flood Ireson, now when Fame
Wipes away with tears of shame
Stains from many an injured name,
Shall not, in the tuneful line,
Beam of truth and mercy shine
Through the clouds that darken thine?

CHAPTER 8

~~~~~~~~

THE SLOOP *TRUMBULL*

On the morning of November 30, 1880, the patrol from the Peaked Hill Bars Life-Saving Station on Cape Cod discovered a shipwreck on the outer sandbar a half mile south of the station. It was the stone sloop *Trumbull*, manned by a crew of five and carrying a deck load of granite from Rockport, Massachusetts, to New York. She had left Rockport the previous afternoon.

Captain David H. Atkins, in charge at the station, launched the lifeboat into the surf and six men soon were rowing out to the wreck.

Upon reaching the scene, Captain Atkins found that he could not approach too near for fear of swamping his craft, so he shouted to the *Trumbull*'s crew to jump into the water, from where they could be picked up. Three of the sailors leaped into the water, but the captain and mate refused to take the chance and remained on the sloop.

The lifeboat returned to the beach with the three sailors, although the captain was troubled by the thought of the two men still out on the sloop. Finally he announced that he was going to make another attempt to rescue them and began his second trip. All went well until he reached the sloop, when the boom and loosened main sheet of the *Trumbull* caught the lifeboat and overturned it.

The surfmen clung desperately to the bottom of the boat, but their leader, Captain Atkins, weakened by his efforts earlier in the day, gave up and sank to his death. Two surfmen, Elisha Taylor and Stephen Mayo, followed him shortly afterward. Three others began the long swim to shore, where they were hauled out of the water by the man on patrol, John Cole.

The ocean almost always performs the unexpected, and the incoming tide brought a moderating wind that allowed the stone sloop to free herself from the dangerous Peaked Hill Bars and continue her journey on down the coast. But the captain and mate of the *Trumbull* must have carried to their dying day the realization that had they obeyed the captain of the lifesavers and jumped for the lifeboat, the second trip of the surfmen would not have been necessary.

Later the same afternoon Captain Atkins' own son helped to recover the bodies of the three drowned men. As he carried his father's remains along the beach, a heartbroken but proud son knew that his father had died carrying out the stern code of the Life-Saving Service.

CHAPTER 9

LONGFELLOW AND THE *HESPERUS*

The wreck of the *Hesperus* is forever associated with the Maine coast—incorrectly. Of course, there are reasons for this misunderstanding. The actual craft in Longfellow's poem "The Wreck of the *Hesperus*" came from Wiscasset, Maine, and she was named *Favorite*, not *Hesperus*. Longfellow, using poetic license, changed the story to make it more dramatic for his readers.

One of the most entertaining visits I ever made to the Craigie House in Cambridge, where Longfellow lived for many years, took place on the day I was allowed by the poet's grandson, Henry Wadsworth Longfellow Dana, to examine the diary in the family vault where Longfellow's journals are kept. Many of us have read the ballad "The Wreck of the Hesperus," and I quote below some of the twenty-two stanzas he wrote:

> It was the schooner Hesperus,
>   That sailed the wintry sea;
> And the skipper had taken his little daughter,
>   To bear him company.

Blue were her eyes as the fairy-flax,
  Her cheeks like the dawn of day,
And her bosom white as the hawthorn buds,
  That ope in the month of May.

                *   *   *

Down came the storm, and smote amain
  The vessel in its strength;
She shuddered and paused, like a frighted steed,
  Then leaped her cable's length.

"Come hither! come hither! my little daughter,
  And do not tremble so;
For I can weather the roughest gale
  That ever wind did blow."

He wrapped her warm in his seaman's coat
  Against the stinging blast;
He cut a rope from a broken spar,
  And bound her to the mast.

                *   *   *

And fast through the midnight dark and drear,
  Through the whistling sleet and snow,
Like a sheeted ghost, the vessel swept
  Tow'rds the reef of Norman's Woe.

                *   *   *

She struck where the white and fleecy waves
  Looked soft as carded wool,
But the cruel rocks, they gored her side
  Like the horns of an angry bull.

                *   *   *

At daybreak on the bleak sea-beach,
  A fisherman stood aghast
To see the form of a maiden fair,
  Lashed close to a drifting mast.

The salt-sea was frozen on her breast,
    The salt tears in her eyes;
And he saw her hair, like the brown sea-weed,
    On the billows fall and rise.

Such was the wreck of the Hesperus,
    In the midnight and the snow!
Christ save us all from a death like this,
    On the reef of Norman's Woe!

I have always enjoyed reading Longfellow's poems aloud, especially before an open fireplace with the burning logs crackling and a storm raging outside. "The Wreck of the Hesperus" is one of my favorites. Therefore, whenever I visited Gloucester, I enjoyed climbing over the rocks leading to Rafe's Chasm. From the chasm itself, I would look over at Norman's Woe in the general direction of Gloucester's harbor. Then I would try to remember as much as I could of the poem and shout it aloud so that the verses would mingle with the roar of the heavy surf at that location.

As time went by I wasn't satisfied merely to look at the reef from a distance, and one day I went over to Ten Pound Island Light where Keeper Edward Hopkins allowed me to take his motorboat and cross the bay to land at the reef itself. I recall one incident in particular when young Ed Hopkins, Richard Clark, and I spent the afternoon exploring the ledge. On the seaward side of Norman's Woe, we found a great pulpit with a cavelike depression under it. Richard climbed to the top of the rock, and I photographed him against the sky. After that pleasant afternoon I was determined to learn all I could about the poem by Longfellow.

It was the following year that I visited Henry Wadsworth Longfellow Dana at Craigie House, where he took me down into the family vaults to see his grandfather's diary and journals. There we read the entries that told in detail what was in

ongfellow's mind before he wrote "The Wreck of the Hes-
erus." Mr. Dana had already done considerable research into
he background of the story itself and was able to give me
everal bits of information never published before. A short
ime later I reviewed all of the newspapers of that year of
839 and was able to piece together the true story of the
Iesperus.

Henry Wadsworth Longfellow wrote "The Wreck of the
Iesperus" as a result of the series of terrible hurricanes that
wept New England within a two-week period during the
nonth of December 1839. The first two weeks of that Decem-
er had been unusually mild, suggesting September or Octo-
er weather, but at midnight on December 14 snow began to
all heavily, and the wind veered to the southeast. Boston be-
ame a temporary island because of an unusually high tide
weeping across what was then known as Boston Neck. Before
he storm hit Gloucester, there were sixty schooners swinging
t anchor in the harbor. During the hurricane seventeen were
roken into kindling wood, three sank at their moorings, and
wenty-one others were pushed ashore. When the gale went
lown, the remaining nineteen were still at their moorings, but
nly one had her sticks or masts still in her. Forty lives were
ost around Gloucester alone, but the worst disaster took
lace at Pigeon Cove, where twenty persons from one schooner
vere drowned. Not until 1898, when the steamer *Portland*
vas lost, was such a storm recorded.

Of course, the next day the columns of Boston's newspapers
vere crowded with tales of the storm. Since the *Morning Post*
vas Longfellow's favorite, it was probably in its pages that he
read the story of the gale. I quote from the December 17,
1839, issue:

The Gale—On Sunday morning, about 3 o'clock, a
N.E. snow storm commenced, occasionally intermingled

with heavy showers of rain. . . . The height of the gale was between half past 3 and 4 o'clock on Sunday, but fortunately had subsided considerably about 6 P.M. and continued moderate nearly an hour, when it recommenced and veered to the Northward. . . . At 11 P.M. on Sunday night, the gale was as high as at any period since its commencement and so continued until daylight when it somewhat abated. This second gust drove the schooner *Hesperus*, at anchor in the stream, from her moorings against the ship *Wm. Badger*, at the North Side of Rowe's Wharf, which parted her lines, and both drove up the dock together.

The *Hesperus* drove her jib boom across the street into the third floor of a building, and her bowsprit was soon carried completely away.

In the same column of the *Post* that carried the account of the *Hesperus* and the *Wm. Badger* is the following news from Cape Ann:

> *Disasters at Cape Ann*—We have conversed with a gentleman who left Gloucester this morning, from whom we learn that the destruction of life and property in the vicinity has been very great. Our informant saw seventeen dead bodies lying on the beach. Among them was the body of a woman, found lashed to the windlass bits of a Castine schr. Two of this vessel were also lost.

That Tuesday night, writing in his diary, Longfellow mentions both the storm and the incidents associated with Gloucester. He also refers to the *Hesperus* but does not indicate that he realized the *Hesperus* was wrecked inside Boston Harbor. The excerpt from his diary follows:

> Tuesday, Dec. 17—News of shipwrecks horrible, on the coast. Twenty bodies washed ashore near Gloucester.

One female lashed to piece of a wreck. There is a reef called Norman's Woe, where many of these took place. Among others the schooner *Hesperus*. Also the *Sea-flower* on Black Rock. I must write a ballad on this.

Later, the *Post* carried a correction in the story of the woman washed ashore lashed to the wreck of a Castine schooner. As it turned out, the woman, Mrs. Sally Hilton, fifty-five years old—no "maiden fair"—had been lost from the schooner *Favorite* of Wiscasset,* not from a Castine schooner, as had been previously reported.

The second of the triple hurricanes hit the coast on Sunday, December 22. During the gale, the brig *Pocohantas* crashed against Plum Island several miles north of the place where the ship *Deposit* had hit in the hurricane of the week before. Two people from the *Deposit* had drowned; eleven aboard the *Pocohantas* were lost. Then came the third hurricane, said by many to be the worst of all. It struck with terrific fury on December 27, causing widespread damage. In Boston the ship *Columbiana* went completely through the Charlestown Bridge and demolished the drawtender's house on Warren Bridge.

On the night of the third storm, Longfellow sat up until one o'clock smoking by his fireside. I quote from his journal:

> Suddenly it came into my mind to write the ballad of the schooner *Hesperus*; which I accordingly did. Then went to bed but could not sleep. New thoughts were running in my mind; and I got up to add them to the ballad. It was three by the clock. Then went to bed and fell asleep. I feel pleased with the ballad. It hardly cost me an effort; flowed easily from my pen. It did not come to my mind by lines, but by stanzas.

* The wheel of the *Favorite* has been preserved by an insurance company in New York City.

The disparity between the true story and Longfellow's account of it should not detract in the least from our pleasure in "The Wreck of the Hesperus." Longfellow had a perfect right to convert a fifty-five-year-old woman into a "maiden fair" for poetic purposes and to utilize the ship and locale that most appealed to his imagination. But for those of us who enjoy the story behind the poem, it should be remembered that the *Hesperus* was wrecked at Boston during the hurricane, and that it was from the Wiscasset schooner *Favorite* that the body of Mrs. Sally Hilton was washed ashore—possibly at Norman's Woe, but probably on the mainland.

Sidney Perley, the New England storm historian, said that upwards of three hundred vessels were wrecked and a million dollars' worth of property destroyed, with more than 150 lives lost, in the three December hurricanes of 1839.

In 1878 Longfellow journeyed to Gloucester and went out to Eastern Point for a very special reason. He found a heavy fog on his arrival. Returning home, he wrote in his journal the significant lines with which I end this chapter:

> I did not stay long enough at East Point to see the fog lift and Norman's Woe rise into view. I have never seen those fatal rocks.

CHAPTER 10

~~~~~~~~~~~~~~

ST. ELMO'S FIRE

St. Elmo's Fire has lately come into prominence because several pilots of airplanes and many masters of ships have seen the elusive glow close at hand.

John R. Herbert, who has studied the phenomenon for many years, tells me that under ordinary conditions St. Elmo's Fire is fairly harmless, but that under certain circumstances it can ignite flammable gases. Mr. Herbert, while flying with his son Robert from Boston to Miami in February 1972, actually saw St. Elmo's Fire moving inside the plane's cockpit, lighting up the instrument panel in spectacular fashion. A reddish color, somewhat similar to the glow of a short circuit, bounced from place to place.

In January 1974, Mr. Herbert's other son, John A. Herbert, was able to help me record the words of Jörgen Jensen, a flyer for the Scandinavian Airlines System.

Chief Navigator Jensen informed me that "the jets are usually able to avoid the electrically charged clouds, but I have seen St. Elmo's Fire a few times at the nose of a DC-8. On the propeller aircraft operating at lower levels, St. Elmo's Fire was much more frequent. From the time when I was stationed in Rome and flew the Far East with DC-6's, I remember a great number of occurrences over India. The propellers were a very impressive sight when lighted with St Elmo's Fire."

John A. Herbert himself observed several demonstration of St. Elmo's Fire while flying in Thailand.

John R. Herbert also mentioned that for a while St. Elmo' Fire was considered a possible cause of the explosion of the dirigible *Hindenburg*; later indications, however, suggested sabotage.

A technical explanation of St. Elmo's Fire is offered by the United States Government Hydrographic Office:

> When the charge on the aircraft exceeds the dielectric strength of the adjacent air, the accumulated charge leaks off, resulting in a corona discharge. Under some conditions this becomes visible, when it is called St. Elmo's Fire. This can sometimes be seen at the wing tips, nose, propellers and the extremities of the vertical and horizontal control surfaces.

The 1943 edition of the *Encyclopaedia Britannica* tells us that "St. Elmo's Fire is the glow accompanying the brushlike discharges of atmospheric electricity which usually appear as a tip of light on the extremities of pointed objects such as church towers or the masts of ships during stormy weather. It is generally accompanied by a crackling or fizzing noise."

There are those who believe that many of the flying saucers seen through the years could be written off as instances of this natural phenomenon. In my opinion, however, the possibility of St. Elmo's Fire and an unidentified flying object being one and the same is remote indeed.

The mysterious light of St. Elmo's Fire, whether atop a church steeple, on the masts and spars of ships at sea, or on airplanes, has always interested mankind.

Quintus Horatius Flaccus, or Horace as we have come to

now him today, was born in 65 B.C. Even then what we all St. Elmo's Fire was observed and talked about. In describing the conditions surrounding this phenomenon, he offered the following in his *Carmina*:

> Soon as their happy stars appear,
> Hushed is the storm, the waves subside. . . .

In this thought Horace does not agree with Longfellow, who, centuries later, stated that St. Elmo's Fire meant foul weather. Pliny the Elder, in his *Natural History*, speaks of the sight of

> . . . during the night-watches of the soldiers, a luminous appearance, like a star, attached to the javelins on the ramparts. They also settle on the yardarms and other parts of ships while sailing, producing a kind of vocal sound, like that of birds flitting about. When they occur singly, they are mischievous, so as to even sink the vessel, and if they strike on the lower part of the hull, setting them on fire.

In Columbus's journal of his second voyage we read that

> On Saturday, at night, the body of St. Elmo was seen, with seven lighted candles in the round top, and there followed mighty rain and frightful thunder. I mean the lights were seen which the seamen affirm to be the body of St. Elmo. . . .
>
> Whatever this is I leave to others, for, if we may believe Pliny, when such lights appeared in those times to Roman sailors in a storm, they said they were Castor and Pollux.

Writing on his voyage from Goa in 1588, Linschoten informs us that

> the same night we saw upon the main yard, and in many other places, a certain sign, which the Portuguese call *Corpo Santo*, or the holy body of the brother of Peter

Gonsalves, but the Spanish call it *San Elmo*, and the Greeks (as ancient writers rehearse, and Ovid among the rest), Helle and Phryxus. Whensoever that sign showeth you the mast, or main yard, or in any other place, it is commonly thought that it is a sign of better weather. When they first perceive it, the Master or Chief Boatswain whistleth, and commandeth every man to salute it with "Salve Corpo Santo," and a *miseracordia*, with a very great cry and exclamation.

In Antonio Pigafetta's history of the voyage of Magellan we find this account:

In stormy weather we frequently saw what is called the Corpo, or St. Elmo. On one very dark night it appeared to us like a brilliant flambeau, on the summit of the mainmast, and thus remained for a space of two hours, which was a matter of great consolation to us during the tempest.

At the instant of its disappearing, it diffused such a blaze of light as almost blinded us, but the wind ceased immediately.

At another time Pigafetta said, "In this place we endured great storm, and thought we should have been lost, but St Elmo appeared, and immediately the storm ceased."

A storm at sea on July 24, 1609, hit a fleet bound for America. One of the craft was the *Sea Venture*. The account of William Strachey, secretary-elect for Virginia, describing the storm was later read by William Shakespeare, who is said to have used the description in *The Tempest*. I quote excerpts from Strachey below:

During all this time, the heavens look'd so blacke upon us, that it was not possible the elevation of the pole might be observed; not a starre by night, no sunnebeame by day was to be seen. Onely upon the [third] night Sir George Sommers being upon the watch, had an apparition of a little round light, like a faint starre, trembling, and streaming along with a sparkeling blaze, half the height upon the mainmast, and shooting something from shroud to shroud. . . .

Halfe the night it kept with us, running sometimes along the maine yard to the very end, and then returning. . . .

The superstitious seamen made many constructions of this sea-fire. It might have strucken amazement.

An unusual event concerning St. Elmo's Fire occurred in Quincy, Massachusetts, a dozen or so years ago. News Editor Richard Carlisle of the Quincy *Patriot Ledger* recalls that he and his family were sitting in the living room of his home at the head of Whitwell Street near the Quincy City Hospital one night when a fireball of St. Elmo's Light came out of the chimney, rolled across the room, and snapped into nothingness near a radiator, vanishing completely.

It is believed that the poet Longfellow saw St. Elmo's "stars" during a voyage returning to New England from abroad. This is a quotation from his "Golden Legends."

> Last night I saw St. Elmo's stars,
>   With their glimmering lanterns all at play,
> On the top of the masts, and the tips of the spars,
>   And I knew we should have foul weather today.

CHAPTER 11

~~~~~~~~~

FORBES AND THE *EUROPA*

Many buildings of downtown Boston around the general vicinity of Washington Street still contain, in the upper rooms above the first floors, literary treasures of value. Early in February 1975, while exploring on the fourth floor of a relatively ancient building at 5 West Street, I came across a torn, mutilated manuscript wedged into the secret drawer of an old desk that at the time was overflowing with books. In that West Street building were almost a third of a million volumes that bookseller George Gloss had crowded together, but he knew nothing of the background of the manuscript I had discovered.

I studied the readable fragments of the manuscript, which apparently was written in the year 1850. Essentially, the material told of a particularly unfortunate shipwreck that occurred on June 27, 1849, in which well over a hundred persons lost their lives. There had been a collision between the mail steamer *Europa* and the emigrant carrier *Charles Bartlett.* What more than interested me was the mention in the manuscript that a resident of Boston, Mr. R. B. Forbes, saved lives by leaping overboard and bringing back victims of the disaster.

I wondered if Captain R. B. Forbes, who had lived in Milton, Massachusetts, could have been the same man mentioned in the manuscript. I had written about Mr. Forbes back in 1944 in my *Romance of Boston Bay*, but I didn't remember the details of the story.

Studying through *Romance* that night, I came across my mention of Forbes' first voyage, taken when he was six years old. I also had written that later he was one of the heroes of the Irish grain famine of 1847 when he crossed the ocean on the *Jamestown* in fifteen days with a load of grain for the starving inhabitants of Ireland. For years afterward Irish children were named Forbes, Boston, and Jamestown.* I had not mentioned the *Europa* disaster, however.

Forbes had written a book, *Notes on Wrecks and Rescues*, and I decided to read through my copy for mention of the *Europa*. When I finished it several hours later I had found not a word of the accident, although the book is meticulous in listing scores upon scores of wrecks. I decided it was a reasonable assumption that if he didn't mention the *Europa*, he couldn't have been aboard.

Evidently the question of whether or not Forbes had been on the *Europa* was weighing on my mind more than I realized. A few nights later, when I returned from giving a lecture at Pease Air Base in New Hampshire, I indulged in far too much of a midnight snack before bed. I then experienced a dream. During the dream my senses told me that I was in the midst of a nightmare involving Robert Bennet Forbes and a person named Crosby. I also realized in the dream that I'd probably forget it on awakening, and my subconscious mind was demanding that in some way I write it down.

Mumbling to my wife, Anna-Myrle, the words *Crosby* and *Forbes*, I promptly went back to sleep. In the morning Anna-

* My own great-grandfather, Captain Richard Henry Keating, now buried at Calcutta, India, was master of a similar grain-carrying craft that same year. As he entered the harbor of Cork and guided the *Jenny Pitts* up to the pier, hundreds of grateful Irish men and women knelt on the wharf in prayers of thankfulness.

Myrle explained to me that she had written down *Crosby* and *Forbes*.

I began thinking about the name Crosby, and remembered that not long before that time Editor Arthur Morris Crosby of the Nantucket Historical Association had sent me a shipwreck story he had written for his association's quarterly. Could it have been of the *Europa's* collision? Then I recalled that Editor Crosby's article had been about the 1952 shipwreck of the tanker *Pendleton*, whose shattered bow can still be seen, in 1976, off Chatham.

I began to ponder again. My thoughts turned to the great-grandson of R. B. Forbes, Henry Ashton Crosby Forbes, who is now in charge of the Robert B. Forbes Museum in Milton. Talking with him, I explained what I wished to know about his great-grandfather. I found that he could solve my problem.

Yes, the Mr. Forbes mentioned in the manuscript was indeed Captain Robert Bennet Forbes, and in an earlier book Forbes had written fully about the *Europa-Bartlett* disaster. His comments on this terrible marine accident follow, taken from his book *Personal Reminiscences*, published many years before his later volume on rescues came out.

I sailed on the 20th June, 1849, in the *Europa*, Captain Lott, for England. On our way to Liverpool, we met with a fearful experience. On the 27th June, while running at full speed in a thick fog, we ran into the American ship *Charles Bartlett*, Captain Bartlett.

The collision occurred about 3 P.M. I was reclining on my couch in the forward cabin, where I had gone to accommodate Mr. Augustus Thorndike, and to get rid of a lot of small children, who made day and night hideous by their squallings. I felt a sudden shock, and knew at once that we had struck an iceberg or a vessel.

I hastened on deck, and on arrival there I found a scene

of horror and confusion which beggars description. Rushing to the port bow, where the ill-fated ship was in the act of heeling over and sinking, and where lay the wreck of our fore-topmast with all the sails attached, I looked over and saw the crew and the passengers filling the fore and main hatchways in a general rush to get on deck. The afterhatch and the side of the ship abreast of it were crushed in, the steam was blowing off with a noise that drowned the shrieks of the people.

Our ship, with all the sails on the mainmast drawing, was forging ahead slowly. All our people were at the bow, trying to save the other crew and passengers. Seeing that I could do nothing there, I rushed aft on the port side to endeavor to clear away a boat.

Only two or three servants and firemen were near, and they seemed to be paralyzed. While trying to clear the boat, I saw a woman and a child come up just abaft the port-sponson. I jumped down, crying out for a rope, and by the time one was thrown to me, a man appeared clinging to a piece of timber. The rope was thrown over him, and he was hauled up more dead than alive.

By this time, the ship had drifted over the woman and the child, who were lying face downwards without any signs of life; and realizing that I could be more useful on the weather side, I mounted and ran over to the sponson just in time to see a man moving slowly by.

I cried out for a rope, and, one being thrown to me, I jumped for him; and, as the ship at the moment rolled to windward, I succeeded by a desperate effort in getting it round him, and taking a turn or two round its own part I contrived so to hold it that, as the ship lurched the other way, we were jerked out of water, against the ship's side, and when the ship came back we went under again.

I cried out whenever above water to "haul up," "haul

up"; but it appeared subsequently that the rope I had hold of was fastened to the side below the gunwhale, probably a short main-sheet hooked into a bolt in the bends, and considerable delay ensued before another rope was bent on to it, and we were hauled out of water.

In the meantime, I had taken in more than was agreeable and had become somewhat tired of holding a slippery hitch with the weight of two men hanging to it; so that at the moment when we were fairly out of water I could hold on no longer, and down went my man.

I cried, "let go!" and went again under water, but could not reach him. By this time, one of the boats came round the stern, manned by the third mate, a couple of sailors, and some firemen and stewards. Seeing my situation, they took me in. I seized an oar, and we pulled off to windward where the debris of the wreck could be seen, among which I perceived some persons struggling for life.

Approaching one of them, I being at the bow-oar, I laid it in, and, seizing a boat-hook, made fast to his clothes and pulled him on board. While doing this, the boat fell off before the sea, and not being very well handled, by the time we got her going in the right direction, another man disappeared.

We pulled round for a short time seeking for more, but seeing none, and those we had requiring immediate attention, and the ship nearly out of sight in the fog, we pulled for her and soon got on board. Before taking me in, she had picked up the man I had been aiding, and one or two others.

We immediately turned our attention to restoring these apparently drowned persons, and with the help of the ship's surgeon and Mr. Francis Peabody, who was very efficient, all save my first man were brought to. Every means was resorted to, and I think if he had any life left in him it would certainly have been rubbed and rolled out of him by our unscientific manipulations.

The man who was hooked up came out all right, and was very grateful. The *Europa* did not leak, and after clearing away the wreck of the top-mast, and hoisting up the boats, we pushed on again.

Only one woman out of about forty was saved, and not a single child out of about the same number. One poor man was nearly frantic over the loss of wife, six little ones, and all his earthly possessions. The passengers generally were of the better class of Germans.

It is a singular fact that nearly or quite all the watch below of the *Bartlett* crew were saved, and nearly all the watch on deck were lost. Most of those saved sprang for the bows and bowsprit of the steamer, Captain Bartlett among them; and most of the forty of the immigrants saved were hauled in over the bows by ropes. About one hundred and thirty of the steerage passengers, and eight or ten of the crew, went down with the ship. I can only account for the loss of the watch on deck, by supposing that they turned their attention to saving others, while the watch below, coming up half asleep, sprang for the steamer.

The one woman, Mrs. Bridget Conroy, who was saved, was hauled in by a bowline. A stout blacksmith was hauled up by one arm, during which process some one caught him by the leg, and the strain was such as to pull his shoulder out of joint. Great exertions were made to set his limb, but as he would not take ether, it could not be done, so that he was taken into Liverpool in great suffering.

Immediately after the accident, a committee was formed, electing Mr. Bates as its chairman, and Mr. Peabody secretary, for the purpose of giving a tangible form to the benevolence of the gentlemen and ladies on board. Subscriptions to the amount of £352 5s. were collected on the instant.

By the latter gentlemen, we were politely favored with a full report of the accident and the whole proceedings, up to the close of the collection of the subscriptions.

At one of the committee meetings on board the *Europa*, the following resolution passed unanimously:

That we have witnessed, with feelings of intense interest, the bold and rapid movements of Captain Forbes, of Boston; that his self-sacrificing and daring leap into the sea to save the passengers of the "Charles Bartlett," commands our admiration; and we rejoice that these deeds were performed by the missionary of the "Jamestown."

The following statement was given of the unfortunate collision by Captain Bartlett:

The "Charles Bartlett" was a first-rate ship of our hundred tons register. She left the Downs from London, bound to New York, on the 14th June, with a general heavy cargo, of about four hundred and fifty tons weight, and one hundred and sixty-two passengers in the steerage, one cabin passenger, and fourteen souls of the crew; had fine weather, with light easterly winds, up to the 19th. From that time to the 27th, had S.W. and W. winds and foggy weather.

At noon it cleared up a little; observed the latitude 50 48 N., and estimated the longitude at 29 W.; all well on board, and every thing looking prosperous. Soon after noon, a dense fog set in, wind W. by S., ship heading to the N.W., close hauled, all sail set. At three o'clock, ordered a good look-out from the topgallant forecastle; also directed the man at the wheel to look sharp to windward. At 3.30 P.M., being on the weather side of the poop deck, heard a rumbling to windward like distant thunder; turned my ear to windward, and my eye to the horizon. The man at the wheel, noticing that I was listening, looked to windward and cried out, "Sail ho!" I at once saw what I supposed was a ship about one point forward of our beam, about four hundred yards distant. I ordered the helm up, thinking she did not discover us, and that we should have time to clear her before she could come into contact. All hands shouted at the same time to alarm the ship, and I ordered the bell to be rung, and called to the ship to "port her helm," as I saw that was the only chance of escape. There were nearly one hundred passengers on deck at the time.

All was of no avail; for, in one minute from the time we saw the ship, she was upon us, going at the rate of twelve knots, striking us abreast of the after mainshrouds. The crash and the terrible scene which ensued I am not adequate to describe. I was knocked to leeward with the man at the wheel. I recovered myself in a moment, shouting for every person to cling to the steamer as their only hope. I caught hold of a broken chain on the bow, and hauled myself up, shouting at the same time to the crew and passengers to follow. I had barely time to get on the steamer's bow; and, while getting up, I noticed that her bow was into the ship within a foot of the after-hatch, and that she was stove clear to the lee side, and that full twenty feet of her side was stove in.

There must have been nearly fifty persons killed by the collision, and every exertion was made by Captain Lott, his officers and crew, and the passengers on board the steamer. Unfortunately, only about ten were saved by the boats; the balance, making thirty-three, more or less, saved themselves by hanging to the bow. The steamer lay by the scene as long as there was any hope of saving any. Of the crew, Mr. Thomas Parker, of Charleston, S.C., aged twenty-two years; George Parsons, of Portland, Me., aged eighteen years; and William Rich, of Gravesend, England, aged twenty-five years, were lost. A list of the passengers and crew saved will be found in the public prints. We were most hospitably entertained by the captain, officers, and passengers of the steamer.

I will notice that all due exertion was used by Captain Lott, and officers and crew of the "Europa," as well as all the passengers. I particularly observed one passenger using the most noble exertions; I saw him let himself overboard, and clench a man in his arms, and, finding him dead, let him go. I next saw him on the bow of a boat, hauling a man from under water with a boathook, who was afterwards restored to life on board. I afterwards found that person to be R. B. Forbes, of Boston.

I cannot express myself as I feel for the noble and generous conduct of all on board in contributing to the wants of the surviving sufferers, and for the sympathy felt by all, particularly by the ladies.

Yours, with gratitude,
WILLIAM BARTLETT.

INDEX

INDEX